KICKING EVERY BALL

To Paul
Best Wishes
Up the Swans!

Nov 2008

To my family,
Roberto, Amor, Antonieta, Josep Francesc, Pau, and Beth
for putting up with football throughout my life

KICKING EVERY BALL

My Story So Far

Roberto
MARTINEZ

with Peter Read

First impression: 2008

The publishers wish to acknowledge the support of
Cyngor Llyfrau Cymru

Cover photograph: Darryl Corner
Cover design: Y Lolfa

ISBN: 978 1 847710 857

Published, printed and bound in Wales
by Y Lolfa Cyf., Talybont, Ceredigion SY24 5HE
website www.ylolfa.com
e-mail ylolfa@ylolfa.com
tel 01970 832 304
fax 832 782

Contents

Foreword

It is a great thrill and privilege for me to write the foreword to
Kicking Every Ball by my very good friend Roberto Martinez. We
first met in our early teens when he was at Real Zaragoza and
I was on the books of Barcelona. We played against each other
many times in the Spanish Youth League and as time passed,
respect for each other's footballing abilities grew into friendship.

When I was with Manchester United, Roberto was playing for
Wigan Athletic and we would meet up regularly after training in
a coffee bar or restaurant in Manchester to discuss tactics and
put the football world to rights. He also helped me settle into
the English culture and find my way around the English kitchen
and cuisine. I have two sisters and since the development of that
strong friendship in Manchester, I feel that Roberto is the brother
I never had. We had keys to each other's houses. He was Best
Man at my wedding and is godfather to my son.

While he was playing for Chester City, he went through a period
of self-doubt about whether he should become a manager. He

loved playing football so much; he was not sure whether he wanted to sacrifice the chance of playing again in order to be a manager. He knew that the challenge at Swansea City would be too demanding for him to combine management with playing.

It was while we were discussing his next move that we had one of our very few differences of opinion. I believed it would be very difficult to manage a team where, as a player just a few months before, he had been out sharing jokes and meals with members of the squad. Roberto thought that the closeness he had established with the players would be an advantage, not a disadvantage, as he knew all their strengths and weaknesses as footballers. He also felt he knew their emotional and psychological make-ups. In the end, of course, he was proved right and moving back to Swansea City as their manager was an excellent decision for him, the club and the fans.

Roberto has been so successful because he is a thoughtful and intelligent manager. He was exactly the same as a player. On the field he would never run without a reason. Every move he made was thought through and had a purpose. He has brought that same attitude to management. He has also instilled a similar perfectionist and professional viewpoint into his players. He has never drunk alcohol or smoked and he expects a commitment to healthy living from members of his team. In the build-up to games nothing is left to chance and he encourages professional footballers to eat and live sensibly.

Football is Roberto's life. When I have a day off, I must admit, I take the whole day off, away from the game. Roberto, on the other hand, is still living and breathing football on his free day. As a player he would spend it running and training in the gym. Most summers my family spend ten to fourteen days on holiday with Roberto and Beth. Since taking his new life in management, his summer time has reduced to four days and although we all enjoy a relaxing time together, Roberto will still make time to phone his chairman and keep in touch with what is happening at the club.

What he has achieved at Swansea City as a manager is fantastic, although not unexpected. I know that he will do everything he can to achieve Premiership status for the club. It will not be easy. Sadly, money is a huge factor in determining whether or not clubs progress in the modern game.

Of the twenty-four clubs in the Championship, there are probably eighteen with more money at their disposal than Roberto and Swansea City. Despite this I believe he will give his all to try and achieve this goal. He has already proved that he has a clinical eye for attracting good players to the club. His signings have been excellent because he is not just concerned about the playing abilities of potential signings. Roberto is also deeply interested in the psychological aspects of a player. Will he be afraid on the big stage and fail to perform? How will he fit in with other members of the team? Through careful and inspired scouring of the lower leagues in Spain and other countries, Roberto has landed players who have served the club well.

I suppose that having spent twenty-five years of my thirty-four years in Spain, I feel, in spite of my Dutch passport, half-Spanish, especially as my wife and children are Spanish citizens. I am proud of what Roberto has achieved for Spain, for himself, for Swansea City and the other clubs for whom he has played. He is a positive, helpful individual, always prepared to support and encourage his friends. I am so glad to know him and outside of my family, I can consider him the most important person and influence in my life.

Jordi Cruyff

Introduction

Thirteen years have now passed since I left the comfort of my native Spain. That's a big chunk of anyone's life but, as you can imagine, it is an eternity in a footballer's life. During that period I have experienced a few shocks in culture and lifestyle as well as in football, where the biggest lesson to be learnt was that football is a matter of opinions and beliefs. There is no right or wrong.

The Spanish have always followed the British game closely and have a respect for the league and the country that invented the game. In Spain the English league is known as the 'Cathedral of Football'. I arrived in the English league with Wigan, open-minded and full of excitement about stepping into the unknown, but I never expected to find such a cultural difference between two footballing nations. During my time here I have discovered a huge difference in the way the game is played. Huge influences from many different markets have helped the British game to develop the Premier League – the best club league in world football at the present time – as well as the most structured and professional lower league set up within the game. In Britain I have met many of the game's characters, huge personalities who have had to develop and adapt into a more professional role. Their survival in today's modern day dressing room is a characteristic of the British game.

Over the past thirteen years there has also been a big change in the lifestyle of the different areas of Britain in which I've been fortunate to live. When I arrived in Wigan the British city centre was typically just a work environment and the majority of the population lived in the suburbs. But gradually these city centres have become more cosmopolitan, with more of a European influence. The work environment has now also become a living and social space, with many and varied options in terms of restaurants and their wide-ranging cuisines, shopping areas and entertainment centres.

I have spent the best part of the last five years living and working in Swansea, south Wales, where I can feel and see many similarities with the way we live in Catalonia. Both Wales and Catalonia are very proud small nations, used to battling to maintain their identity, where sport plays a major role in their self-expression. Both countries are very passionate, friendly and proud of their heritage and the institutions that their colours represent.

Catalonians will be very jealous of the Welsh being recognised on the sporting front as a country in their own right and allowed to compete in official competitions such as the European Championships and World Cup. It is a battle that the Catalonians are slowly trying to win while playing their own 'unofficial' games on a yearly basis, displaying their own pride through the medium of sport.

That sort of passion and determination is something we have worked hard to display at our own Liberty Stadium in Swansea, to give us a boost towards winning football games. It made a huge difference throughout our title-winning campaign last season and, already this season, as we have moved up to a new level with Championship football we have created some special football occasions where you could feel the pride of our fans enjoying the new era. The team has produced performances and results that have added new chapters in Swansea City's history, with wins against the likes of Leeds United in League One, Cardiff City in the Carling Cup and against early league leaders Wolves in the Championship. Our progress has made many fans proud of Swansea City Football Club, of the city of Swansea and of Welsh football.

As a football person I am very fortunate to be involved in a sport that is so important in terms of national pride and the role that it plays in the daily lives of local people and their families. This spirit spills over into the Swansea City dressing room, where the Catalonians and Basques within our squad, along with the Dutch, Irish, Trinidadians, Argentinean and English, can easily identify with the way life is lived in this part of the world, and that has helped them both as individuals and football players to settle in Swansea.

It's been a great challenge for our Welsh players to host all the nationalities, and bed them into our city and football club; a great responsibility to introduce all the different cultures into the Welsh way of life, making them feel at home and able to be competitive on the pitch with the help of our passionate fans. In turn Swansea City Football Club benefits from having very focused and hungry players who will give everything to win football games for our football club.

The next few chapters are intended as a reflection of a life where happiness depends on winning or losing over 90 minutes. A life based on kicking every ball.

Roberto Martinez

October 2008

CHAPTER ONE

February 2007

The Road Back To Swansea

I<small>T WAS A WEEK</small> I will never forget. On the Tuesday night I played for Chester City in League Two against Bury. As I walked out onto the Deva Stadium pitch I remember thinking, 'This may be the last game I ever play for Chester.' The next day I was meeting Swansea City chairman Huw Jenkins to talk about the manager's post there. For days the possibility of going back to Swansea had been playing around in my mind. Having been dismissed at the end of the 2005–06 season after three-and-a-half years at the club as a player, I felt there was unfinished business I needed to resolve. I also knew everyone at the club, I knew the fans, I knew the way they were thinking and I also knew what they wanted as a club. As I thought through the possibilities of taking the reigns at the Liberty Stadium, I believed that my philosophy of playing would be right for Swansea City.

In that game against Bury I was determined to put in

a good performance in case it was my last appearance in the blue and white stripes of Chester. My determination paid off as I was voted Man of the Match. Four days later, on the Friday morning, I trained with the club, and then had a chat with the manager, Mark Wright, to discuss the next day's match away to Swindon. After the meeting I found a message on my answer machine. It was Huw Jenkins telling me that the job was mine and that they wanted me to move down there as quickly as possible. I was in my Chester tracksuit and all the players were in the bus outside the stadium waiting for me. I couldn't move as I was waiting for confirmation from the Chester chairman that the deal was approved. At that precise moment I wasn't sure whether I was a Chester City player in League Two or the manager of Swansea City in League One. Eventually the phone rang and I was told everything had been confirmed, the compensation had been agreed, and that the club wished me all the best for the future. The bus left without me, and it took me a couple of hours to make the transition from my Chester tracksuit to moving to Swansea as the club's manager.

That game against Bury turned out to be more than just my last game for Chester. It was also my last game as a professional footballer. As I would be taking over as manager on February 23, 2007, outside the transfer deadline, I would not be able to play for Swansea for the rest of the season. Throughout my career I had always advised fellow players to continue playing for as long as their bodies would allow. When Swansea expressed an interest in me becoming their manager, I had to think long and hard about the consequences. The approach came as a shock as I had to face the question earlier in my career than I had expected – I was just thirty-three years old. It had always been my aim to play for as long as I could. Even when you get to that point where you realise the body might be struggling to keep up with the high demands of playing at a high professional level, I had always told myself and advised friends in the game to keep going. Nothing can beat the thrill of actually playing football, but I soon realised that, as Swansea was such a big club, it would demand my total attention and I wouldn't be able to give it if I were playing and managing. This belief, plus the impossibility of playing for the rest of the season, combined to bring my playing career to an end.

My father, who was a professional footballer before becoming a manager, had played until he was forty-three years old. As a player I had looked after my body, never smoking or drinking, and had always been careful to eat the right food. Even though I had always wanted to move from playing to management I had assumed that would happen in my early forties, yet here I was in my early thirties taking charge of a club which meant a lot to me. The whole incident taught me that in life you can't plan what is going to happen next. When something unexpected comes along you have to assess whether it is right for you. Looking back I now realise that this development happened at the right time and I made the correct decision.

As I drove down to Swansea to start my new job I felt like I was going back home after a short seven-month period. It seemed I'd been away on loan and all of a sudden it made sense that I had never had a proper chance to say goodbye to the fans. Strangely, when I met Huw Jenkins on the Wednesday at a hotel near Chester, I hadn't fully realised that it was an official interview. He had contacted me and asked whether I would consider the job, and I had responded positively, but even when I walked into the room I thought it was just an informal chat where we would share ideas and visions for the club. There was a sign on the door saying Swansea City Football Club. He then told me that they were considering other people. I later discovered that they had a shortlist of four or five others, including Gary Megson and Dean Saunders.

I was looking forward to the new challenge and to putting my philosophy into action. Football is a results industry, but I don't believe the result can ever make your style of play irrelevant. To me it is important that the route to the result is attractive. We need players with a desire to win football games, with a winning mentality and technically ready to cope with the demands of playing for Swansea City. You have to find the chance to score rather than chase it. As well as the skill, you need a clear understanding of the game and a clear control of the tempos of play with the possession of the ball. As a manager I want to rely on the talent of the player, not on percentage football, to win a game. I believe this approach is vital. I will never subscribe to the view that as a manager you can take any way to a win because that can only bring success to the football club in the short term. It doesn't allow you to build and grow something for the future. Within League One I felt that there were about 16 clubs where my philosophy wouldn't be welcome as the fans would not accept it. They would want to win quickly and with a direct approach. I knew that Swansea was different. The fans wanted to get back to the Golden Years of John Toshack and Alan Curtis, when the team played beautiful football. I knew that by getting rid of the wrong attitudes and tactics, and by following this philosophy, there was a place for me within the management of the club, and it was a case of seeing how far we could go.

For these reasons I realised there was a certain type of player I wanted. They had to fit in with the aims of the club and be hungry for success. I didn't want players who may have lost some of their motivation or desire to win games consistently. They also had to be technically comfortable on the ball and possess a winning mentality. In a desire to make a name for themselves, they would have to be prepared to go through that wall that marks the difference between achievement and mediocrity. As a manager it would be my responsibility to motivate the players both individually and as a team. I suppose anyone can pick a team, but not everyone can manage it, treating each player with respect and getting the very best out of them.

I knew that some people outside the club thought it would be difficult for me to make the transition from player to manager. The perception persists that if you know the players too well you will struggle to assert your authority. Personally, I think you cannot know them too well. The more information you have on individual members of the squad, the easier it is to motivate them and help them through tricky periods in their careers. I decided there was a need for us all to be honest with each other. The hardest part of my new role would be the fact that the friendships I had enjoyed as a player would have to be put on hold. You cannot manage a player if he is a close friend, but the information you have gleaned from such a friendship is vital in helping a player reach his potential.

In addition to deciding on the style of play and the best way to motivate players, I also realised that it was vital to consider the training schedule. Being a footballer must be a passion not a job. You are a professional footballer twenty-four hours a day. You need to look after your body so that it is always in pristine condition. This belief has shaped what we do at the club. We give the players two meals a day. The training is a well-planned method which helps the players to be comfortable on the ball. We are keen to make the players tactically aware, so that they are adaptable, depending on the type of opposition they face. I never want to manage a team that can only ever play in one style.

When I took over at Swansea I was also at pains to point out that in the lower leagues there were ways to play other than thumping the ball up field to your target man. We had to work really hard to be ultra dimensional and have different approaches to playing different teams. It was also important, from the point of view of the players' lifestyle, that they mapped that out for themselves. My job is to give them information so that they can make the decision for themselves. I would never stop a player doing something in his life which he thought was right for him. They all know that I am teetotal and I will tell them why my lifestyle is important for me and why I think having a healthy approach to the way you live can often add four or five years onto your playing career. If you are a dictator, they do what you tell them when you are around and then behave in a completely different way when your back is turned. That is not my style.

On February 24, the day after I was unveiled as the new manager, I travelled to meet the team and to watch them play at Yeovil. The Swans were three places adrift of the play-off positions and they had won only one of their last eight games in all competitions before the kick-off at Huish Park. It was interesting going back into the dressing room after an absence of a few months, as I had left the club for Chester at the end of the previous season. That day, as I watched the players lose 0–1 to Yeovil, there were many things that worried me. I didn't like the players' body language and I didn't like their lack of enjoyment of being on the pitch. I knew there were many things that the boys could do but weren't doing. Part of me felt that we were a long way from being play-off challengers, but I also felt encouraged, as I believed there were many things we could put right straight away. Having played with most of the players the previous season, I knew what they were capable of doing. I realised I had to bring them back to a place where they could once again enjoy their football but also be very competitive.

I had just a couple of days before a Tuesday night fixture away to Rotherham. We worked on a few things in training and straight away I saw a difference in the performance at Millmoor. Although our 2–1 victory suggests it was a close encounter, the result didn't tell the whole story. We played with great composure and controlled the game, with Rotherham scoring a consolation goal in the dying minutes. The contrast between Yeovil and Rotherham was huge. I realised after the Yeovil match that the players were mentally dry. They were not enjoying their game and the expectations of the fans were starting to wear them down.

Playing for Swansea City is hugely demanding. In

many ways I believe the pressure is similar to playing for a big club like Real Madrid or Barcelona. The fans expect you to win every match. This was illustrated the following season when we lost a Carling Cup match to Premiership side Reading. We pushed them all the way and only lost in extra time, yet there were lots of fans who were complaining about the result! After the Yeovil match, I realised that the players had to rediscover the joy of football and be freed from the pressure of the fans' expectations. They had to walk onto the pitch looking forward to the game. As a player you cannot take for granted what is going to happen out there on the pitch. Mentally you have to be in the place where you enjoy the pressure of wanting to win. It's important that the pressure comes from yourself, not just from other people. It was vital that the mental attitude was corrected, but I also felt that, technically, they were not playing to their strengths. I needed to give them a little boost in every single department.

Football players will always be exposed to negative views. We are a family club and the players will bump into fans as they go shopping or as they move around the city. The press can also weigh heavily upon them. At Carlisle in the 2007-08 season, at half time we were losing 1-0 at home. In the second half we were outstanding and won 2-1, yet some members of the press claimed we were lucky. It's as though some people dwell on the ten bad minutes instead of the eighty where you were brilliant. As a club I felt that for too long we had been seeing the bottle as half-empty instead of half-full. That mentality stops us from developing. We are surrounded by a passionate group of fans, and we need to channel that fire so that it intimidates the opposition rather than us.

After the Rotherham game I felt that we had changed things within a few days. We were still not where we wanted to be in terms of performance, but we had made a start. In football you need time to build a solid base from which you can progress. I had only 12 games left before the end of the season, which is not a long time, and yet I saw that we were adapting well to the new philosophy.

While we were learning the new strategy, we were still managing to win games. After the Rotherham game, we drew at home to Leyton Orient, but that was followed by three consecutive victories: away to Tranmere Rovers and then at home to Chesterfield and Northampton. That run was followed by an away defeat at the hands of Millwall. Our next game was at Ashton Gate against Bristol City. Although we drew 0-0, it was during this game that I realised how far we had come in a short period of time. We should have won as we had several chances and dominated the game for long spells. They were a first class side and went on to be promoted into the Championship. Talking with them after the game they were very impressed with the way we had performed. That day I saw that we had the winning mentality throughout the squad. It was also good to realise that we could perform against the best away from home. If you can only produce good football on your own ground, then you are going to be a mid-table team, not winners.

After the Bristol game, we took ten points from a possible twelve, drawing away to Bournemouth with victories against Port Vale, Brighton and Carlisle. Just as the Bristol City game showed that we were emerging as a powerful side, the 3-0 home victory over Port Vale was also pleasing. That day we played with great confidence and defeated the opposition comfortably.

Our 2-1 win at Carlisle left us with one game to play, at home to Blackpool. They were the form side in League One. In October they had been languishing in the relegation zone but, by the time they arrived at the Liberty Stadium, they had secured a play-off place. However, despite this, they were well motivated because they knew that if they won, and Nottingham Forest and Bristol City both lost, they would be promoted automatically without having to go through the trauma of the play-offs.

Similarly, we were in an 'ifs and buts' situation. On the same points as Oldham, we were battling with them for the final play-off place. A crowd of 18,000 packed the Liberty Stadium to cheer the side on. At one stage we were 3-2 in the lead. In any other situation we would have won that game, but, having heard that Oldham were beating Chesterfield, we knew we had to hunt another three goals, as they had a superior goal difference. It was a huge ask and in the end we were beaten 6-3, with Andy Morrell, the ex-Wrexham striker, scoring four times.

Although I was disappointed that we had missed out on the play-offs, after the game I was pleased that we had come so far as a team in just twelve games. We had an excellent base on which to work for the next season. We had discovered the areas which needed improving, as well as seeing the strengths in our game. As difficult as that moment was when we realised that our season was over, it was a great pointer to the new campaign.

CHAPTER TWO

May to July 2007

Rebuilding the Squad

A T THE END OF 2006-07 SEASON I brought in ten new players. Some of the players had spent a few years at Swansea and I think some of them were looking for a move. Izzy Iriekpen was one of those who didn't accept our terms and he decided to look for another club. Adebayo Akinfenwa was injured and, despite being offered a new contract, he also left, along with Pawel Abbott and Tom Williams. Willie Gueret joined MK Dons and Ian Craney re-signed for his old club, Accrington Stanley.

I needed to bring in players who were different from what we already had. Within the squad I had players who had fought for the club in 2003 to keep our league status, players like Leon Britton, Alan Tate and Kris O'Leary. These players, plus characters such as skipper Gary Monk, Dennis Lawrence and Andy Robinson, were to form the bedrock of the new team, but we also needed players who could give the club a new dimension.

Many fans were despondent because Lee Trundle left

the Swans for Bristol City. To them he was a hero and a legend who had scored nearly twenty goals in each of the four seasons he had been with us. I knew that we would miss his flair and his ability to entertain the fans, but I also thought that no player should be bigger than Swansea City. I felt that in the past the club had perhaps allowed this to happen. Lee wanted to play in the Championship and as a club we offered him everything we could to try and keep him. We also told him that we believed he would make it to the Championship with Swansea, but it would, of course, be a slower route. Lee felt he wanted championship football sooner, so he signed for Bristol City.

When a player of Lee's calibre leaves a team, you have to prove that you are able to win games without him. I believe it was a sign of a strong football club and a strong dressing room that we were prepared for the new season. We didn't spend any of the money from his transfer straight away and it gave other players in the squad an opportunity to show their character, personality and maturity to express themselves on the pitch, to take the football club forward and to fill important roles in the squad. After Lee moved to Bristol, I managed to get the dressing room together and get the players more determined to fight their way to the Championship.

All the players I brought in had the same desire for success as Lee. They were hungry to win honours with their new club and enthusiastic about their football. They were also at a great age to play. Lots of new names came to the Liberty Stadium, people like Ferrie Bodde, Dorus de Vries, Angel Rangel, Guillem Bauza, Andrea Orlandi, Jason Scotland, Mattie Collins from Fulham, David Knight, Febian Brandy on loan from Manchester United and Paul Anderson on loan from Liverpool. We signed another loan player, Warren Feeney from Cardiff City, who was with us until he got injured in December. In addition, Darryl Duffy, who had been a loan player the previous season, made the switch and signed on permanent terms. We only signed players who fulfilled the new Swansea City criteria; full of desire and hunger to win games on a consistent basis and possessed of the footballing talent needed to play within the philosophy of our football club.

There was a huge turn around in the players. It was quite clear from early on that the players we now had in the dressing room wanted to play for Swansea City. Selling the idea of how good it would be to play for the Swans was easy in respect of some of the players but harder with others. For the last game of the previous season we invited Ferrie Bodde over from Holland to watch us against Blackpool. Similarly, we encouraged Andrea Orlandi to come and look at the facilities. As a manager it is much easier to sell the club and say what direction you want to take it if you are able to have a face-to-face conversation. At that moment you know whether the player you are meeting is a Swansea City player or not.

It was hard work to secure the signature of Jason Scotland. Our club secretary, Jackie Rockey, deserves a huge amount of praise for ensuring that he joined Swansea City. She did a fantastic job in producing a dossier to explain why he should be given a work permit to play for us. She managed to gather several letters of support from charities in Scotland which Jason had helped when he had been at Dundee United. She also explained why we needed to sign him and how he possessed a talent which we didn't have at Swansea City. We had to go to London and present our case. With me at the hearing was my chief scout, Kevin Reeves, and the club's chief executive, Alan Cowie. We had to convincingly deliver the case, which Jackie had prepared earlier, to a panel of six people who would make the final vote on whether Jason could become a Swansea City player. It felt like being put in front of the *Britain's Got Talent* audition, though in this case it was a bit more like *Jason's Got Talent*!

The panel making the decision consisted of ex-managers, personnel from the Football League, PFA and Football Association of Wales, and individuals from the Home Office. We had to present a vision of what Jason's achievements would be with the club. (That is not an easy thing to do with any player but Jason has gone on to prove that our account of him on that day was no exaggeration. And after scoring 29 goals in his first season it was perhaps fair to say that Jason in fact exceeded our claims.) After the hearing we were asked to leave the room and wait outside along with Mike Berry (Jason's agent) in what was a long and anxious forty-five minutes while Jason's future was decided.

With a unanimous panel vote it cost us about £25,000 to sign Jason, and we then went on to pay £60,000 for Ferrie Bodde and £10,000 for Angel Rangel who, in my opinion, has proved himself to be one of the best defenders in all the leagues. Guillem Bauza came to Swansea on a free transfer after very promising spells at Mallorca and Espanyol. I also felt that Mattie Collins, who was captain of the Wales Under-21 team, was a significant capture as he is still developing into an important player.

As I assembled these players I was aware that many of them would not be known to Swansea City fans, but we had been following them for a long time through Kevin Reeves. Kevin had flown all over Europe watching players who could bring something different to the club. Kevin's knowledge of the game is second to none. He shares my vision in finding players not only with talent but with a Swansea City attitude. Kevin has got a sixth sense in spotting talent in foreign markets that is adaptable to the demands of the British game. The human aspect of the player is also well assessed. We had to control many markets where we could be competitive. These include the Scottish, Dutch, Spanish, French and German markets. To control that market you have to be prepared to put in a lot of miles and watch an awful lot of games. Then you have to put in offers for players you feel would fit into the Swansea style of play. Often they are not names in Britain, but you know that they are potentially great performers. The type of players I needed had to be spotted in these markets.

Knowing how I wanted the team to play, it was impossible to get the chequebook out and find them in the British market. If you want to compete in the lower leagues, it is in these markets you have to hunt for your playing staff. It is very easy to be sucked into the huge ocean of the British football market, where landing a player can become a never-ending auction. I believe that it is important for a club to find its own identity and seek raw talent from all over Europe. Such players, coming from different sporting backgrounds, also bring a freshness and new dimension into the dressing room which is good for everyone associated with the club.

Some of the players I have signed have not made as many appearances as others, but this is bound to happen when you have a large squad. What is important is that they have all played a part on a daily basis in the shaping of the team. In that sense I have been very pleased with the signings I made before the start of the 2007/08 season.

There had been huge changes at the club and as manager I had to be understanding of the players. There was pressure on them from both inside and outside the club. Inside there was a new way of looking at things, both mentally and technically, and outside, as the new season dawned, there were expectations that, having just missed out on the play-offs, we would achieve automatic promotion. This belief would cause us difficulties throughout the season. We would have an excellent run followed by a defeat and, after that one reverse, people would start saying, 'That's it. The bubble has burst.' I heard that remark several times and it's a view I don't understand. People have to realise that you are not going to win every game. You may deserve to win every contest, and you must set high standards and perform within those standards consistently, but games can turn on all sorts of things, such as a piece of magic by the opposition or a bad refereeing decision. Sometimes the result can be an unfair reflection of the performance, but out of ten good performances you'll get the rewards you deserve. The ability to react positively and with character to a bad result is always a huge strength in a successful team.

As long as the effort and intention of the players is good, you have to be patient. As I've already mentioned I was somewhat disappointed with the press after the turnaround victory at Carlisle in September 2007. It was a tough challenge against a good side. We had a refereeing decision go against us and, as they were in the lead, they put eleven men behind the ball. Despite their approach we just kept playing and probing until we exposed them and got the result we deserved. As a manager I want the players to focus on the period when they were brilliant, not the brief period where they were struggling. I believe it is important for everyone connected with the club to have that attitude and realise that over a period of ten games we are going to win more than we lose.

After the games against Millwall, Tranmere and Northampton, although we had only lost two games in twenty-one, some people preferred to dwell on the fact that we had not won for three games. This is an attitude I have fought to change at the club. We had a wonderful run of eighteen games unbeaten and, if we had won the next game at home to Millwall, we would have set a new club record for the longest undefeated run. All of a sudden the statisticians were full of gloom.

That season we had to come to terms with the fact that being top of the table, as we were for most of it, brings a new set of pressures. Everyone wants to beat the top side. We had to get together and think about our attitude and remind ourselves that, although we may have lost one, we were still top, so we must be doing something right. As the season progressed we learned the need to group together with our backs against the wall, and fight back with the right attitude.

As we prepared for the challenge of the new 2007/08 season there had been no despondency about the fact that we had missed out on promotion in the previous campaign. We were encouraged that we had almost got to where we wanted to be in a short space of time. We had entered the new season with optimism and enthusiasm as we felt that we were on level pegging with all the other teams in League One.

We worked very hard on our pre-season programme. As far as I am concerned there are two elements to this part of the campaign. The first is to make sure that everyone works hard at finding their fitness level, and the second is to get all the players together so that they get to know each other and gel together as a unit. The way you achieve those two objectives is by exposing the players to different environments. We had three very different settings. Firstly, we worked at Fairwood, near Swansea Airport. Then we went to Sweden where there were no distractions, which meant that I could relate to all the players and set the guidelines for the season. After Sweden we returned briefly to Swansea and then we left for our tour of Holland. These three diverse situations allowed the players to keep pushing themselves. They also ensured that the players wouldn't grow complacent because they kept encountering new challenges. We discovered areas where we had to help each other and spend time on certain aspects of the individual player's game.

In many respects there are different targets for the different elements of the pre-season training. Obviously, in Sweden it was all to do with conditioning and to that end we had one game against Ostersund. It was a good experience for the team; their first taste of eleven against eleven in the new season. With so many new faces in the squad that was an important run out for us. Returning to Swansea, we played several games locally.

CHAPTER THREE

August to December 2007

The Turning Point

A T THE START of every season, fans and the media always manage to create a huge hype about the first game, and our trip to Boundary Park to play Oldham Athletic was no exception. Rightly or wrongly, everyone seems to think that if you win the first game it will set you up for the rest of the season. Such an attitude makes those first three points on offer more important than they actually are. Oldham has always been a tough place to go to in League One. We lost with the last kick of the game. Such a defeat would normally be heartbreaking and lead to lots of negative feelings. In reality, our response to the game was the complete opposite.

Our overall performance was outstanding. The reaction of the Oldham players and staff confirmed that view, as they were amazed how they had ended up with three points. Coming away from that game we knew there were certain aspects of our game on which we would have to work, but on the other side of the coin we could see that there was a lot to make us feel positive. We had brought a lot of new players into the club in the pre-season and they had worked together well. I thought the way we played that day was well above the League One standard. I have never seen a defeat look so positive, and that set us up for the rest of the season. I also felt that the fans were positive at Oldham. It was as if they could see beyond the result, which is something I always want, although I know it is difficult for them because we are in a results business. You always have to have a bigger picture and see the performance first and then look at the result. In that Oldham game, our fans were upbeat. They got behind the team and they enjoyed the performance. The only thing we all wanted to change was the scoreline and that, of course, was the next challenge in front of us.

Every season when the fixtures are published, fans, players and management are always looking for certain fixtures. For us, in addition to Leeds United, the question was when were we going to play Nottingham Forest? As well as the Yorkshire club, Colin Calderwood's team were favourites to win promotion to the Championship. As a club we didn't have to wait long for the answer as Forest were the first league visitors to the Liberty Stadium.

We were looking forward to the game, but I have to admit I was a little disappointed by the encounter. It has to be the most one-sided 0-0 draw I have ever seen! On the other hand, it was pleasing from our point of view as some of the football we played was outstanding. At the same time we realised that we had failed to convert the numerous chances we had created during the ninety minutes. You can't win games without scoring and at the final whistle we were aware that certain things would have to change if we were to be a force in League One. In spite of that, the very fact that Nottingham Forest felt the point they had gained was a great achievement proved that we had to be on the right path. The Forest goalkeeper, Paul Smith, performed heroics on the day and showed why he was to go on to be voted one of the top three goalies in the division, alongside Keiron Westwood of Carlisle United and our own Dorus De Vries. As the game went on, Nottingham Forest seemed to change their tactics and adapt their style of play. They obviously decided to play a more solid game and put as many players behind the ball as possible. When they did that I realised they were paying us an encouraging compliment. As far as we were concerned our performance was a step forward, after the one at Oldham, and without winning the game, I thought we were improving.

Before the league game against Nottingham Forest, we had defeated Walsall 2-0 at home in the first round of the Carling Cup, with goals from Paul Anderson and Jason Scotland. Now we were in action against Walsall once again, this time in the league at their Bescott Stadium. Two goals from Andy Robinson, one of which was a penalty, and another one from Jason Scotland, gave us a 3-1 victory.

After our visit to the Midlands we were at home again, this time against Premiership opposition in the second round of the Carling Cup. The matches seemed to be coming thick and fast even though it was early in the season. In view of the pressure on the players I decided it was important to bring in some reinforcements. For the cup match against Reading I introduced a few new faces to the Liberty Stadium fans. Our pre-season signing from Spain, Guillem Bauza, and local boy Joe Allen both made their first appearance for the Swans. The great performances they gave that night proved to me how strong the squad was. It was also pleasing to realise that whenever players were called upon they were ready to seize the opportunity to impress. To play against a team from the top drawer was a great test for us. To be holding them 0-0 after ninety minutes and the standard of our performance was very pleasing. Although it was disappointing to concede a goal in extra time and lose the tie, there were too many positives from the encounter to be downcast. Reading manager Steve Coppell paid us a huge compliment after the game. He had watched our matches against Oldham and Nottingham Forest and was amazed how much possession we had enjoyed and how we had dominated both games. He also said he had expected a hard battle, but the way we had played it turned out even more difficult than he had anticipated.

I believe the home game against Carlisle United in early

September was a turning point for us. If you look at our record in the Liberty Stadium, it hasn't been the best. Our record up to that point had been one win in two games. If you want to achieve anything in football, then your home record has to be better than that. Looking back, I think what was happening was that we had allowed an anxiety culture to develop. If after an hour we were not winning, the fans would grow tense and that tension would spread to the players. In the game against Carlisle we conceded a penalty to go 1-0 down. After their goal I think we showed an excellent sense of responsibility. The players kept the ball, showed great patience and eventually wore Carlisle down. Once we had subdued them we opened the game up, used the whole pitch and got the right rewards. The fans also played a massive role that day. They got right behind the team as we came back from 1-0 down to win 2-1. In the last twenty minutes you could feel something happening in the stadium. It was as if the fans were turning that disappointment and anxiety into belief. That day made me realise that we had to make the last twenty minutes of every game at the Liberty Stadium the longest in League One football. As we did with Carlisle, we had to be patient and press the opposition in that period where fatigue would help us to break teams down and allow us to win football games at home.

Carlisle was not the only team in the 2007-08 season to treat a visit to the Liberty Stadium like a cup final. All the visiting teams seemed to raise their game, and that factor, plus the expectations of the fans, created the difficulties. At times the two pressures seemed to feed off each other and make it difficult for the team. There were no easy games and, when teams came and organised themselves behind the ball, we found it difficult to break them down until we changed the mentality of the club and the approach of the players to each game. Such a transformation took time, of course.

Following the Carlisle victory we chalked up an away win at Cheltenham, beating them 2-1. Then we visited Elland Road to meet Leeds United. Despite having fifteen points deducted before the start of the season for administration and irregularities, they were riding high after six successive wins under Dennis Wise. Before the game, expectations were high. We wanted to show the highly-fancied team in the division that we were also serious contenders for the number one spot. In a crowd of nearly 30,000 we took 2,500 Swans fans with us and the atmosphere before the game was terrific. Unfortunately, the performance and the result didn't match the occasion. It was the only time in the season where I felt we gave away a two-goal lead without competing. I think playing in front of such a large crowd affected the players, and the way we played fell well short of the standards we had set ourselves. That 2-0 defeat started another learning curve for us as a club. As we chatted after the game we agreed that we would never allow ourselves not to be ourselves when we played in any other ground in the League. I think looking back on that match at Leeds, it was the only game in the entire season where I felt we didn't deserve to win. For the first hour it was as if we didn't understand that, as Swansea City, we should be able to perform in any ground and under any circumstances. Again, despite the defeat, the game acted as a turning point, because after that game for the rest of the season we never underachieved at any other ground.

On our next travels we certainly proved we had learned our lesson. After two home matches against Brighton (0-0) and Swindon (2-1) we went to meet Leyton Orient who were top of the league and undefeated at home. We knew that this game was going to be a test of character, but it was the kind of season where we kept facing such examinations. This was inevitable, not just because we were challenging for promotion, but because we were a new squad, learning new ideas and trying to gel together as a team. We struggled to break Brighton down but, in the Swindon game, showed that we now had that winning mentality. Orient were flying high and we saw the game as an opportunity to put right what we had failed to get right at Leeds. To beat them 5-0 and gain the highest away win in the history of Swansea City Football Club answered the growing criticism and showed our fans and other clubs that we were on our way. Our play won us the Performance of the Week, an honour handed out by a panel of managers including Sir Alex Ferguson. It was not a fluke result. In the early stages Orient created quite a few chances to go ahead, but our defence stood firm. It was a fast open game and we made enough openings to score more than five.

In late November our 1-0 victory over Hartlepool put as at the top of the table.

December was an excellent month. We played like champions and our performances were accompanied by the results they deserved. In previous months we had played well but come away at the final whistle with either a draw or a defeat. Now performances and results were going hand-in-hand and, during that four week period, we looked pretty invincible, scoring 19 goals in five matches. Once we added the performance level to a winning mentality we started to dominate the division.

Up to that moment Leeds were the outstanding team in terms of their results. They were strong, very physical and well organised throughout the team. They were also superb at converting set pieces into goals. Dennis Wise had created a team which knew how to win a game and hold on to leads. Having defeated us fairly comfortably at Elland Road earlier in the season, their arrival at the Liberty Stadium posed a huge test for us. We were still top of the table but we knew that was where Leeds United wanted to be. We needed to prove that we were not Pretenders but had a right to be top team.

Before kick-off a lot of thoughts were running through my mind. It was a game I was desperate to win. Firstly, it was payback time for what had happened in the earlier contest and, secondly, I wanted us to win what would be a battle between two opposing football philosophies. They were an outstanding team and the deduction of fifteen points before the season started had galvanised them into action and brought them closer together as a unit that was ready to fight the world and everything that was against them.

We got into the game slowly and struggled for the first ten or fifteen minutes. After that difficult opening period I thought we played very, very well. Then as we were starting to put our stamp on the game, Ferrie Bodde was sent off. To play for an hour with ten men and beat them 3-2 shows how well we did. That victory meant that we ended the year 2007 at the top of League One. The question we all had to face as a club was, 'Could we stay there?'

CHAPTER FOUR

January to May 2008

Staying On Top

I T IS ONE THING to be the leading team, but it is more difficult to stay in front of the pack. While we were top of the table on the first of January 2008, we wanted to make sure that we were still there on the third of May when the season ended. Results during the month were encouraging in the league, but January 2008 will always leave a sour taste for me as it was the third round of the FA Cup. After a 1-1 draw at home in a bad-tempered match against Havant and Waterlooville, we were given an away tie at Anfield against Liverpool. Everyone at the club was excited by the prospect of a trip to Merseyside. The last time the two teams had met was in January 1990 when the Swans had left Anfield after an 8-0 thrashing. As a team, top of League One and playing excellent football, we were convinced that we could put things right with a much better performance. Unfortunately, we were never to get the chance, as we lost the replay 4-2.

Though the result and the implications of the result

were a huge disappointment, we had to accept that this was not the first time a non-league team had progressed at the expense of a team from the league. We also knew that it would not be the last time such a result would occur. In many ways it adds to the magic of the competition, but we were unfortunate that we were part of that magic for all the wrong reasons. Despite the fact that we approached the tie with the right attitude, there are many circumstances which will help a cup upset develop.

We had played in earlier rounds against Billericay and Horsham in the cup and in both those games we had been called upon to play the worst role, that of the favourites, but had come through with two victories.

In the first encounter against Havant and Waterlooville at the Liberty Stadium, the referee allowed them to be too physical. In the players' minds I think this was a factor and it prevented the game from developing in the fluent way we like to play. At the end of that home tie we knew it was another lesson to learn. During the tie we created twenty-five chances, hit the cross bar three times, had Alan Tate sent off and then conceded the equaliser in the last few minutes.

For the replay we knew that going into their environment was going to be difficult. Even though we conceded three goals in a very short period of time we continued to play our style of football. I still felt we were in the game. We fought back to 2-3 down, but then missed a penalty. We continued to press, hit the cross bar and missed chance after chance. When the final whistle blew, we all felt bitterly disappointed.

We also felt that something had been taken away from us in the home tie. If you play like we did on that day then nine times out of ten, you would win. We also felt aggrieved that in that tie both teams had a man sent off, yet because of the rules of our respective leagues, their player was allowed to play in the replay whereas Alan Tate was not. In the Football League if a player is dismissed in the first meeting, he cannot play in the replay. Unfortunately, that rule does not apply to non-league clubs. This is a situation which I am sure will be changed in the future as it was the first time it had happened in the history of the cup.

As we looked back on the two games with Havant and Waterlooville, we did feel that there were several factors which had gone against us and there was the perception in the club that we had fallen foul of fate. Although none of us felt it at that moment, looking back I am glad we didn't progress any further. The despair became a turning point, and it drove us on in the league campaign. The defeat was a blessing in disguise.

On the weekend we could have been playing Liverpool, we had the long and difficult trip to face Doncaster Rovers who at that time were our nearest rivals. At the start of the game Rovers began brightly. As I watched I realised there was now a great maturity in the team. We weathered the storm and then went on to dominate the game for seventy minutes, something which we had failed to do at Elland Road against Leeds, but had done very successfully away to Leyton Orient. We won 4-0, and that result was an important statement to everyone else in League One. That day we showed that we could play with width and speed. It answered those critics who early in the season had looked at our squad and asked where our target man was. We proved at Doncaster and in many other games that we relied on dimensional play rather than the traditional hit man. Before the game, Doncaster Rovers had been hailed in the media as 'the Arsenal of League One' because of the way they played stylish football. After their defeat, they showed what a good side they were by going on a long, unbeaten run and, of course, they ultimately won the play-offs and gained promotion to the Championship.

We followed the Doncaster victory with another difficult away trip, this time to play Nottingham Forest, still many people's favourites for automatic promotion. It was another severe test for the team. We were going to an ex-Premiership club with a Premiership-sized crowd. We controlled the occasion very well. Once again we were ourselves, played our brand of football and came away with a crucial point in a 0-0 draw. We were confronted with a completely different set of questions from that which had been posed in the game at Doncaster and the home game with Leeds, but, once again, we managed to stamp our authority on the proceedings.

During February we managed to extend our unbeaten run with victory over Oldham at home (2-1); an away point at Crewe (2-2); a 1-0 defeat of Walsall at the Liberty Stadium; a 2-0 success at Port Vale and a 1-0 home victory against Luton Town. The month was also dominated by our appearance in the two-legged area final of the Johnstone's Paint Trophy against MK Dons, who were running away with League Two. Sometimes the cup draw is kind but on this occasion we had faced difficult teams in every round: Millwall (h 3-2); Wycombe Wanderers (h 2-0); Yeovil (1-0) and Brighton whom we beat 1-0 at home in the regional semi-final. We had deserved to progress in every round as we gave good performances over ninety minutes in each game. After the first leg against MK Dons at the Liberty Stadium, I felt it was a bit harsh on the team that we had lost 0-1, especially given the open football we'd played and the number of chances that came our way in the opening stages of the game.

After the setback we were pleased that we had a chance to put things right at Milton Keynes in the second leg, and hopefully progress to the final. We played well and pulled back the goal deficit, but were unable to get a second goal to clinch a Wembley appearance. That meant we had to go into a penalty shoot out which we lost 5-4. When that happens, you know as a manager that you have no control over the result and you are in the lap of the gods.

Throughout the competition I had said that to win the cup you have to be good, but you also have to be lucky. MK Dons certainly had both, as two of their victories on the way to Wembley were after penalty shoot-outs (Swansea and Gillingham). They then went on to beat Grimsby Town in the final. Losing that night at their stadium was a bitter disappointment, especially as our exit from the competition followed a winning result.

On the weekend we could have been appearing in the final at Wembley we gained an excellent 3-1 win at Hartlepool. The night before, Doncaster Rovers chalked up an impressive victory over Nottingham Forest, but our result at Hartlepool put pressure on the Yorkshire outfit and kept Swansea at the top of League One. Just as I was to look back on the Havant and Waterlooville defeat as a blessing in disguise, once the disappointment had eased I began to see that the MK Dons result was another turning point in our season, and that a trip to Wembley could have been a massive distraction to our League One campaign. If we had had a good run in the FA Cup and an appearance in the Johnstone's Paint Trophy final, at the end of the season we may have been looking at another term where we just missed out on promotion. Overall, I think we converted the two massive cup disappointments into positives in our promotion campaign.

Throughout the season the team showed the ability to bounce back after a setback with a convincing win. We did it at Doncaster after Havant and Waterlooville and at Hartlepool after MK Dons. As a football team you will never win every game so you need to cultivate the ability to cope with defeat, get the positives out of each disappointment and resolve to follow defeat with victory. In football your team consists of eleven brains working together. You play with your feet and sometimes the brain doesn't seem to exercise much control over them. Results can sometimes be down to a questionable decision by the referee or an awkward bounce of the ball. What you can control is the spirit in the dressing room to fight back. I think we had that after every bad decision or result. We would come back more determined for the next challenge and that is why we finished where we did.

In early March we defeated Huddersfield away (1-0) to equal the club record of eighteen league games without defeat. We needed to beat or draw with Millwall at home to set a new record. Every manager who brings a team to our stadium is thinking how to defeat us. I think our home defeat to Millwall (1-2) came down to the fact that we wanted to achieve a new club record. In a way we played the occasion and not the game. The fact that we were going for the all-time record of the longest undefeated run in the history of the club seemed to weigh heavily on the players. It was as if they played the ninety minutes too quickly, as if they didn't understand what was needed to win a football match. It was a very disappointing result and also sad that we didn't achieve the record.

At that time, early March 2008, we were entering the final phase of the season where every performance and result matters for every single football club. Looking into that last section of the season from the outside, you would have to say that we were so far ahead in the league that everything was fine. We were working towards our points tally and were confident that it would be achieved. However, from inside the club and looking at the situation from the viewpoint of the fans, we seemed to enter 'the Panic Station'. The period after and including the Millwall match was a tricky one for us because we drew 1-1 at home with Tranmere Rovers and then lost 4-2 away to Northampton Town.

It was another learning curve for us as an emerging team. We had to react maturely and in a level-headed way. We had been saying at that time of the season that, if we could win two more matches, we would probably be promoted. Just because we lost two games, it didn't mean we were going to be relegated. After the Northampton game some were saying we hadn't won in our last three games. What needed to be said to redress the balance was that we had only lost twice in our last twenty-two League One games! We needed to remember that players, fans and staff knew what their roles were and, if we mastered them, then I believed we would achieve what we deserved at the end of the season.

Over the busy Easter period with three games in six days, we stayed on course for promotion and remained in top position. A 2-0 victory at Bristol Rovers was followed by a hard fought 1-1 draw at Roots Hall against a strong Southend United team who were making a late, unbeaten surge for a play-off spot. A 2-2 home draw with Bristol Rovers was followed by the 3-1 defeat of Hartlepool United. After that excellent performance we returned to the Liberty Stadium to play Bournemouth. The Cherries were struggling near the relegation trapdoor as they had entered administration and suffered a ten point deduction. With ten minutes to go, we were leading 1-0 and news from Huddersfield told us that Doncaster Rovers were trailing 0-1.

Over fifteen thousand fans were singing and chanting, celebrating the fact that at long last we were on our way to the Championship. Then in the last few minutes it all changed. Doncaster Rovers equalised at the Galpharm Stadium and, at the Liberty Stadium, Bournemouth scored twice in the dying minutes. The result gave the visitors a lifeline for League One status, and meant that we would have to wait to secure promotion.

That game showed why millions of people watch football every year. It is such an exciting and unpredictable game. Those last two minutes emphasised the exhilarating side of the sport and also proved that football can be cruel. At eighty-nine minutes, with us leading and thinking we were promoted, Dorus de Vries apparently conceded a corner which the video later proved should never have been awarded. We failed to defend the corner, a lapse which led to Bournemouth's goal, and, before you could blink, we were 1-2 down. Given the form that Bournemouth were in, having won seven out of their last eight games, you look at a result like that and wonder if it was meant to be. They certainly showed that afternoon that they were fighting for their lives after all the difficulties of their season. The great thing was that, despite that unexpected setback, we still had a huge margin for error, because of the fantastic season we had enjoyed up to that point. We were determined to put things right at the earliest opportunity and achieve promotion.

Our next game, away to Carlisle, was the ultimate test for such ambitions. Carlisle had the best home record in all divisions of the Football League and they, too, were pressing for promotion to the Championship. It was a Tuesday night and we had a great following from Swansea in the crowd of 10,000. In the first five minutes we hit the cross bar and imposed ourselves on the game. Later on in the contest, we had a goal disallowed and we were so dominant throughout the encounter that, at the final whistle, although in reality we had drawn 0-0, psychologically it felt like a win. Carlisle's Manager, John Ward, was annoyed by the Swans' celebrations at the end of that game and, with four games to go to the final day, he predicted his side would overtake Swansea. He was obviously trying to give his players and fans a boost, but I think any neutral observer would have been convinced that there was a huge difference between the two sides.

That week was very demanding for the fans as they had to make two long trips. The trek to Carlisle was followed by the equally long and tedious journey to Gillingham. The Gills were fighting for their existence, and we knew that we needed three points to clinch promotion. One-and-a-half thousand fans travelled along the M25 and down to Kent and they filled the away stand at the Priestfield Stadium. The atmosphere throughout the game was electric. A draw would not be a good result for either side as both needed to win for very different reasons, and that brought extra tension into the ninety minutes which builds a difficult environment for the away team to play in. However, the support of the Swansea fans made a huge impact in our performance allowing our players to grow into the game and impose ourselves to overtake Gillingham's 1-0 lead. We defended extremely well and had great phases of play as the players began to write a new chapter of history for our club. It was another fantastic performance by the players, which earned us a 2-1 victory and promotion to the Championship.

The result allowed us to achieve the dream which had driven us on for the entire season. After the final whistle there were a lot of emotions spilled by players, staff and fans. It was a great moment and a great place to be, but it probably affected our performance the following Saturday against Yeovil Town at home.

Players are only human and there are times when physically you are desperate to win a game, but not as focused mentally. Having secured promotion the previous week, we knew victory would ensure that we went up as Champions of League One. Yeovil were fighting against the mathematical possibility of relegation. They arrived at the Liberty Stadium determined to salvage at least a point from the game. As the game progressed they showed that they were well organised. They scored with their first real chance and went on to win 2-1. The encounter showed how difficult it is to win games at that stage of the season when almost every team in the division is fighting for promotion, a play-off place or safety from relegation. Despite the defeat, the other results were kind to us and we finished the day as Champions of League One.

In the following match at home to Leyton Orient, the boys were determined to make amends for the previous result. They didn't want to go through the strange sensation of celebrating without a victory, as they'd experienced the previous week. In the first forty-five minutes we played in a way which illustrated the standards we had set ourselves for the whole season. We were ourselves and beat Leyton Orient with a wonderful display and a 4-1 victory.

As a team we were surprised when we discovered that the City and County of Swansea council had organised a parade through the streets to celebrate the fact that we were the champions. The open-topped bus left the Vetch and went through various areas of the city before arriving at the County Hall. It was a great feeling standing on top of the open bus and seeing the thousands of people who had turned out to congratulate us. We travelled in the same bus which was used in 1981 to celebrate John Toshack's team reaching the top division for the first time in the Swans' history. We saw so many happy faces that day and felt that we were once again in the glory years of Swansea City Football Club.

Despite the excitement and euphoria around the club and the city, we were not awarded the League One trophy because of the ongoing Leeds United saga. Before the start of the season the Yorkshire club had had fifteen points deducted and towards the end of the campaign they took the matter to the High Court. Unfortunately, the judges did not give a ruling until Thursday, May 1, just two days before our final match away to Brighton. We were left with a hollow feeling after the Gillingham and Yeovil matches, because technically Leeds could still have caught up with us if the court awarded them the fifteen points. It was a strange situation, one which I had never encountered before in any European league. Throughout the history of football there have always been clubs who will appeal against a Football Association ruling. In this situation, to have allowed it to roll on until one game before the end of the season was difficult to understand. Almost half of the clubs in the division were affected by the action Leeds took, as it impinged on those who were hoping for automatic promotion and those who were battling for a place in the play-offs. It threw up so many problems that I am sure it will be the first and last time such a crisis develops. I am convinced that the Football League will bring in legislation to prevent a club appealing so late in the season.

Compared to some of the other teams, we were lucky. We knew that we were promoted. Carlisle, Doncaster Rovers and Nottingham Forest were all fighting for second place and automatic promotion, and they didn't know if it was still open. We managed to get around the difficulty and the only disappointment was that we were unable to celebrate with the trophy in front of our fans. As a player you don't have many opportunities throughout your career to receive a Champions trophy and to celebrate those emotions with your fans and sadly that was taken away from our players. I understand why Leeds United appealed; I think every club would have done the same.

On May 1, 2008, the decision went against Leeds and two days later we defeated Brighton 1-0 and our points tally meant that Leeds would not have overtaken us if they had been awarded the fifteen points.

We took nine hundred fans to the Withdean Stadium. The Brighton club were very accommodating, allowing us to have a party with our fans at the end of the game to celebrate a truly fantastic season*.

---

*For full results for the 2007-8 season, see Chapter Ten, page 166

CHAPTER FIVE

February 2003 to May 2006

Playing for the Swans

ROM THE HEADY HEIGHTS and excitement of the last chapter with promotion to the Championship, we turn the clock back to my first experience of Swansea City. I joined the club as a player in February 2003 when we were in a delicate position. Near the bottom of the bottom league, we were facing the ignominy of slipping into non-league football. I was playing for Walsall in the Championship, when Colin Lee, the manager, approached me to say Brian Flynn, the Swans' manager, had been on the phone and I had the option to join them.

I went down to meet Brian at the Ramada Jarvis Hotel. I studied all the information my agent had given me and I was very impressed by Brian Flynn. He sold the club to me and I loved the challenge ahead. 'We've got a huge task on our hands,' he said, 'but Swansea City is a massive football club.' Of course, I had heard of the glory days under John Toshack and I knew that they had a proud history but were now in danger of disappearing from the Football League.

I was impressed by the fact that Brian wanted to get out of trouble by playing football. Many British football managers think that the only way to pull away from the threat of relegation is through a bunch of physical players who go for route one and percentage play. Such an approach would be a contradiction of all I had attempted as a player. When he invited me to join the battle, I couldn't wait.

I moved down from Walsall on the Thursday night but, unfortunately, my new career as a member of the Swans' squad didn't get off to the best of starts. The details of the agreement were not as they should be, and I had come back to Walsall. I was psychologically pumped up for the game against Lincoln City on the Saturday, but, instead of training for that game with my new team mates, I had to drive back to the Bescot Stadium on the Friday, still a Walsall player. I had three uncertain days wondering where my career was going next. Then on the Tuesday I received a phone call to say that everything had been sorted, so I drove down to Swansea once again, this time as one of their players.

I trained with them in readiness for the Friday match against Rushden and Diamonds. They were flying high at the top of the table and were, without a doubt, the best team in the division. The match was to be televised on Sky, and it was to be billed as a real Goliath at home to David. Fortunately, in front of the television audience, we played extremely well and drew 1–1. In many ways we should have won the game, especially as we had a goal disallowed. I knew at the end of that contest that we had a great chance to play ourselves out of trouble.

Brian Flynn had brought in some key players on loan from Premiership clubs. Leon Britton arrived from West Ham United, Alan Tate from Manchester United and Marc Richards from Blackburn Rovers. Kevin Nugent had also been brought in from Leyton Orient. In an attempt to save the club there had been a huge turn around of personnel. Leon had been at the Vetch for six weeks before my arrival. He had played extremely well and picked up a few 'Man of the Match' awards, but, unfortunately, had not been on the winning side.

Just a few nights before the trip to Rushden and a day after my signing, I sat and watched the Swans lose 2-1 to non-league Newport in the FAW Cup. At the end of that game I thought we had a huge mountain to climb, but as often happens in football we looked a completely different side the following Friday, and at the end of that game I allowed myself to feel slight optimism. Looking around I realised that there were enough experienced heads to see us through. We had players like Roger Freestone and Kristian O'Leary, who, along with Lee Jenkins, loved the club and lived for it. There were also other talented players, such as Michael Howard and Jason Smith. Lenny Johnrose, who had also been brought in by Brian from Bury, was playing in midfield alongside Leon Britton and myself.

The three of us clicked very quickly and formed a good partnership and understanding. We were very different types of players, but between us we managed to give good service to the forwards, James Thomas and Kevin Nugent. On the wing we had Jonathan Coates, a left-footed player, who on his day was a world beater. It was a master stroke of Brian Flynn to sign Coatesie. He had been playing for a Conference side while training with us. The manager could see that we needed a left-sided player and had a word with him after one of the training sessions. His re-signing for the Swans was to play a huge part in our subsequent survival. It was not just his playing skill which helped us through that difficult season. He was a very lively character who had a totally different way of looking at life. It's wonderful to have such a person in the dressing room when you are facing difficulties on the field. His humour lifted the tension and pressure that was around the place. He came in at the right time and, in crucial games such as Rochdale and Hull City, performed really well.

I believe Brian Flynn and Kevin Reeves had seen me play a few times for Wigan Athletic against their team Wrexham. I had been involved in several close battles between the two teams. I have always admired the way Wrexham try to play football, and Brian Flynn had a similar philosophy. Just before I signed for Swansea City, he came to watch me in a Walsall Reserves fixture against Sheffield United, and that was obviously when he decided

My first Zaragoza top, Lobo Diarte No 9.

Sunday meant football, and my sister had to join in.

Proudly showing my new Tango football, the ball for Spain '82 World Cup.

At home in Balaguer.

At 38, my dad still had another five years of playing left.

Quick to collect my dad's medals from my mum.

Church before football on Sunday with my sister Antonieta

Plaza Mercadal, main square in Balaguer

Mascot for the day in my dad's team.

Captain of the school football Sala team.

Before kick off, Carmelites v Bellcarie under 8s.

Receiving trophy from the city councillor.

Collecting my trophy after competing in my first 24-hour football Sala tournament.

Real Zaragoza under 18s.

First competitive 11-a-side game, aged 9.

Again with Zaragoza.

Top left: *In Real Zaragoza digs with 1st team captain Xavi Aguado.*

Top right: *Real Zaragoza versus FC Barcelona, 90/91 season , keeping a close eye on Jordi Cruy.*

Above: *Real Zaragoza under 19s Super League.*

89/90 Season. Real Zaragoza v. FC Barcelona, Spanish under-19 Super League.

After signing for Real Zaragoza, age 16.

*Real Zaragoza 'B'
debut, 1991.*

*Real Zaragoza 'B' at
Romareda Stadium,
17 years old.*

*Spanish 'Copa Del
Rey' game against
Betis at Romareda
Stadium, under 19s.*

Winners of Montey tournament in Switzerland '91 with Real Zaragoza.

Last game for FC Balaguer before joining Wigan Athletic, 94/95 Season.

Top left: *first season in the British game, 95/96, at Springfield Park.*

Top right: *first home friendly with Wigan Athletic, 1995 v. Lancaster (Lancashire Cup).*

Middle left: *celebration time after last game of 96/97 season, achieving top spot in the league above Fulham.*

Above: *Ewood Park, FA Cup versus Blackburn Rovers, January 1998.*

The Three Amigos, with the FA Cup.

Reunion of the Three Amigos, with Dave Whelan.

Top left: *first ever game in the British game versus Burnley in Lancashire Cup, '95.*

Above left: *home league game versus Plymouth at Springfield Park.*

Above right: *before the game at Springfield Park.*

Top left: *August 07 league debut against Gillingham.*

Above right: *first time in the PFA Team of the Year.*

Left: *versus Blackpool 97/98 season.*

Below: *Wembley, Football League Trophy final with Wigan Athletic.*

Above: *Player of the Season in the 95/96 campaign, presented by Joe Parkinson (Everton).*

Above right: *with Isidro Diaz showing the trophy to the fans.*

Right: *with my assistant Graeme Jones and the trophy.*

Below: *Springfield Park crowd after winning the title in the 96/97 season.*

Top: *Champions 96/97, after a long hard season.*

Right: *Motherwell in SPL.*

Below: *versus Dundee Utd, no football to be seen.*

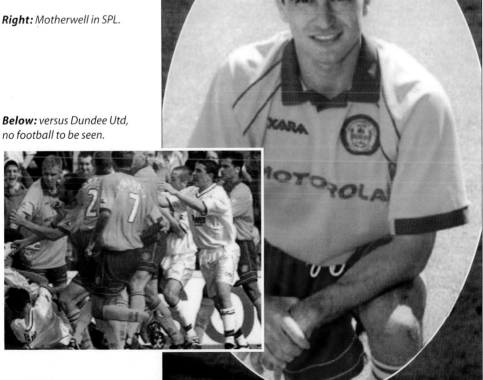

In Walsall colours in warm up before Reading game.

Walsall debut against Wolves at Molineux.

At Bescot Stadium against Reading, 2002/03.

to sign me. We had nineteen games left to save the club. We had a very good start with an encouraging return of results and got ourselves into a position where we could probably afford to lose a couple of fixtures. That happened at Easter with an away defeat to Leyton Orient and a home loss against Exeter City. Exeter were our main rivals and, like us, they were fighting to avoid that final relegation spot. With that result we put ourselves into a terrible mess. We were suddenly in that situation where it wasn't just a matter of us getting points; we needed other teams around us to slip up.

I suppose at the end of the season we got what we deserved, because the way to escape from trouble was to play football. That was what we believed as a football team, and I think we gained our rewards because of that philosophy, which went right through the club.

The support we had at the Vetch was a terrific help, and the closeness of the terraces to the pitch meant that the ground was fantastically intimidating for the opposition. One match that proved that for me more than any other was against Oxford United. When they came to the Vetch they were near the top of the table, but we managed to beat them 3-2 in what turned out to be a very entertaining game of football. I believe that was a turning point in the campaign. We started to think we might be safe. A lot of the optimism was due to the crowd and the atmosphere they created at the ground. I am glad to say that eventually we were able to transfer that raw excitement to the Liberty Stadium.

After the Easter fixtures we had two tough games to finish the season, one away to Rochdale and the other at home to Hull City on the last day of the season. Two teams would be relegated into the Football Conference league and there were four teams trying to avoid the drop: Carlisle United, Exeter City, Shrewsbury Town and ourselves.

In every league campaign when you are trying to achieve something, there is always one game which is as important as a cup final. For us that match was away to Rochdale. Marc Richards came on as a substitute and scored with his first touch. A little later he had a one-on-one against their keeper but he missed the chance. With a couple of minutes to go to the final whistle, we were 2-1 up and Rochdale were awarded a corner. From the corner, one of their players had an open goal and he missed it. As well as that victory, the other results went our way that day. It meant that, if we could beat Hull in the final game of the season at home, we would be safe and Exeter would go down with Shrewsbury. After that Rochdale game I really believed that we would stay up. Until that game there had been a huge build up of pressure felt by the fans and the players. Until our win at Spotland, our destiny was out of our hands. The future depended on other teams helping us. The victory over Rochdale and other results meant that once again we were in control of where we would be playing our football next season.

When I joined Swansea, all the football newspaper reporters and radio and television pundits were telling me that Swansea had no chance of remaining a Football League club. The question everyone was asking was, 'Who is going to go down with Swansea City?' At that time Shrewsbury were just three points outside the play-off positions and no pundit would ever have predicted that with a week to go to the end of the season they would already be condemned to the Conference. It just showed the different dynamics of two clubs. One had gone into free fall, whereas we had enjoyed a tremendous points return from our last few games. Psychologically our position served as a wake up call to remind us that football doesn't respect history.

Despite our perilous position for most of the season, there was a good atmosphere within the club. Under Huw Jenkins and the new Board of Directors there was a feeling that the club could and would turn the corner and that in the future the good times would return again. There was also an excellent feeling among the players. We bonded well together and there was a strong belief that all that mattered was to save Swansea City. This was unusual because we had a lot of loan players in the squad. For a loan player it would be very easy for him to switch off and say, 'Very soon I'll be going back to my club.' Such an attitude would result in him not trying his best. This never happened among our squad and I think the fact that there were so many loan players helped rather than hindered the team's progress.

Having temporarily left our clubs, we were all living near each other in Swansea and quickly became attached to each other. After training, we would all go to Paco's, the Spanish restaurant in St Helen's Road. Without him knowing it, the owner played a huge part in saving the football club. When I signed for the Swans he wrote to me at the club and encouraged me to visit his establishment if I ever fancied Spanish food. Very soon the other players joined me. As a footballer it is important to eat well and we were certainly never disappointed. In many ways our regular visits were just as much a means of therapy as a place to eat a good meal. We would get together around the table, share the problems and look forward to the next game. The record books will say that our survival as a club depended on a good result against Hull City. We players know that it was also down to Paco's Spanish Restaurant!

Throughout the season there had been times when, despite my belief that we would ultimately be safe, there were a couple of occasions when I found it difficult to sleep. I suppose the two key matches were when we lost at home to Carlisle United in late March and Exeter City at Easter 2003. But now we had got to the last day of the season and needed a victory.

In that vital game against Hull City we took the lead through a James Thomas penalty but then found ourselves

2-1 down. It was a unique game where you could sense and smell the occasion. It was a huge contest for the Swans. We were playing against arguably one of the best teams in the division, who, with more or less the same squad, went on to win promotion in successive seasons.

We made two mistakes in defence which allowed Hull to score. Then Neil Cutler made the save of the season from Ben Burgess to keep us in the contest. If we had gone 3-1 down, it would have been very difficult to come back. On the pitch we could feel the tension of the crowd. They probably felt that their great club was just an hour away from falling into the world of non-league football. That world class save from Cutler gave the players belief. We had played some good football at home and we knew that was what we had to do now. James Thomas scored near the end of the first half and when we went in to the dressing room at half time drawing 2-2, we knew we had a great chance of winning.

We could see that Hull were frustrated as they came off the pitch. They had played well in the first forty-five minutes and were now feeling down because we had drawn level with them. Despite the fact that I and some of our other players felt confident, there was a lot of tension in our dressing room. Our goalkeeper, Roger Freestone, couldn't stand still or sit down. He was pacing around the room with his cup of tea demanding to know why we weren't winning. 'There'll be no more wages for us if we can't win this one,' he was saying. He chivvied us all to try and find a solution and make sure we won. Normally at half time the players relax, take plenty of fluids and listen to the manager's assessment of how the game has gone and whether there is a need for any tactical changes. That day it was far too emotional for a normal fifteen-minute break. Players just wanted to have the win. We were losing sight of the fact that in situations like that you have to remain calm and play the game. The best place to be was on the pitch because at least out there you can influence the situation. You can get on the ball and make things happen.

During the interval, we also learned that Exeter City, who were playing Southend United at home, still had twenty minutes of the first half to play. Brian Flynn had kept this fact from us while we were playing. It was a dreadful situation in that it could have given them an unfair advantage if we had finished and they knew what they had to do. They were obviously trying every trick in the book to influence the afternoon, but by then we knew that we only had to win to be safe.

As soon as we got back on to the pitch in the second half, there was a feeling among all our players that the worst part of the day – being behind to Hull – had gone. In the second half we scored two quick goals, one from Lenny Johnrose and the other a wonderful chip from James Thomas. In the last forty-five minutes, Hull City had a couple of long-range shots, but, otherwise, we were completely in control. Their striker, Stuart Elliott, is an excellent player who has played at international level for Northern Ireland. I had played with him at Motherwell, and I believed it was important not to let him near the goal. In the second half we really did control him and the rest of their forward line. Being ahead 4-2 with fifteen minutes left, we knew we were almost there. We were shouting to each other to keep the pressure on Hull and telling each other to run at the goalkeeper and harass him. For those last few minutes, we were able to play with pure enjoyment. The final whistle was the greatest relief of my life. It was a very different feeling from my reactions at Gillingham in 2008 when we clinched promotion to the Championship. At the Priestfield Stadium our reaction as a team was that we had completed the job well and now it was time to celebrate, as we deserved to be promoted into a higher division.

After the Hull match, I think it was more a case of a job well done, but we got away with it! Despite my mixed emotions, that day taught me how vital it was to have a dressing room where everyone bonded together. If individual players don't believe that it is an honour to play for Swansea City, then they can never fulfil the expectations of those who love the club.

From the beginning of February 2003 when I joined the Swans to that vital day on May 3, 2003, when we played Hull City, every player had to shoulder his responsibility and realise how important it was to keep the club afloat. Survival meant so much to thousands of individuals, not just in the Swansea area but in many parts of the world. People had written to us from Moscow and other places in Europe wishing us all the best for our final game of the season. That season taught me that Swansea City have fans all over the world. We received letters wishing us success from as far away as Australia and Canada. The fans would write saying they had followed the Swans for thirty or forty years and a victory over Hull would mean everything to them and their family. We put those messages on the dressing room walls, so that we would see them when we went out to play and when we came back in after matches.

We all had to forget about our own personal careers and realise that we had been charged with the task of achieving for Swansea City Football Club, rather than for ourselves. In that dressing room for the Hull match, every player except Andrew Mumford was out of contract at the end of the season. In a situation like that it is very easy for individuals to lose focus and not worry about the plight of the team. It is easy for them to think about their summer holiday and wonder where they will be playing the following season. Mercifully, it wasn't the case at the Vetch, and that's the reason why we stayed up in the Football League. Everyone cared so passionately about Swansea City.

Looking back on those difficult times, I still believe that

if we as a bunch of players had not experienced the therapy of sharing our hopes and our worries at the Spanish restaurant, then we would not have survived.

When we started the next season, 2003-04, we were on fire. Brian Flynn kept the same footballing philosophy and the same set of players. He added one or two significant signings to the group which had rescued the Swans. Lee Trundle signed from Wrexham and the football we played at the beginning of the campaign was something special. We were regularly scoring three or four goals each game and we got to the top spot in the division very quickly. Unfortunately, we were unable to maintain that high standard of play and we finished the season in tenth place. After the horrors of the previous season, tenth was a good position.

During that season the league was so tight that almost every team flirted near the bottom at some time. Swansea were the only team to stay away from any hint of relegation, mainly because of our good start. There was further upheaval when Brian Flynn was dismissed and Alan Curtis took over as caretaker manager. Kenny Jackett was appointed as Brian's successor and, after his appointment, we had six straight defeats. It was a difficult way to finish the season after the early promise of the first six months.

From a personal point of view the next season, 2004-05, was a very difficult one. I don't think my style of play suited

Kenny Jackett's plans. I had enjoyed a good pre-season and was happy with my fitness levels and performances on the tour of Holland. In our first league game at home to Northampton I was replaced after fifty-five minutes, and I knew as I walked off that I wasn't going be part of his vision for the future.

From then on I faced a huge challenge. I was out of the squad completely and had a massive fight on my hands to win my way back into the team. In the next game away to Rochdale, I was not even in the sixteen. I had to work very hard, as I understood that I was being nudged out of the team. It would have been a very easy option to walk away and find another club, but I wasn't prepared to do that. I knew that I could still give a lot to the Swans. While I was on the sidelines, we played in a cup match against Queens Park Rangers which we lost 3-0. I felt tremendous support from the group of travelling fans who chanted my name throughout the game. Their support was so important, because, although I was facing a tough time, I felt I still had a lot to give. I also resolved that I would try and work my way back into the team for the sake of those wonderful fans.

Since the traumatic season where we had to fight to stay in the Football League, I felt that I had become attached to the fans. It was obviously a two-way feeling, as we had joined together to try and save the club. A respect had grown up between us which made me determined to play my way through the difficulties. When the picture looks bleak it makes me more determined to turn things around, instead of walking away.

I stuck at it and battled my way back into the team, so that, by the end of the season, along with Sam Ricketts, I had probably played more minutes than anyone else. After a few bad results, I was called back into the team to play away against Cambridge United. We won 1–0. That was followed by a 1-0 victory over Lincoln City at home. We then played at Yeovil where we gained a highly creditable point.

My return to the team coincided with a very good spell in the league, and it saw us climb back up into the top positions. Despite this encouraging period, I was still convinced that the manager did not really want me. It was nothing to do with personality clashes. We never argued or fell out, but I was just conscious that, to fit his style of play, he wanted a different player in my position.

We continued our good form and, towards the end of the season, we were in a play- off position. Our final home game of the season was against Shrewsbury Town and, more poignantly, it was our last league game at the Vetch before we moved to the Liberty Stadium. It was a strange day, unlike any other game. As part of the build up to the match, there was a lap of honour made by ex-players.

Marquees had been erected outside the ground,

some of them selling meals and others hosting auctions for memorabilia, so that the atmosphere was more like a carnival than a professional football match. While all this was going on inside and outside the ground, we knew as players that we had to stay focused on the game. We had to win, so that we would have a chance of automatic promotion in our final game away to Bury. As a player, I didn't really enjoy the occasion. It was a very nervy game, with many tricky moments that we had to get through, but we eventually won.

On the last day of the season, we drove to Bury knowing that we must win to have any chance of securing the third automatic promotion place. We also needed Southend United not to win their last game at Grimsby. During the season, Southend had been way out in front, but had been distracted by reaching the Freight Rover Trophy Final at the Millennium Stadium where they lost to Wrexham. Despite their blip in form, we still expected them to beat Grimsby, as the home team had nothing to play for.

The atmosphere in the game against Bury at Gigg Lane was terrific, as we had taken a huge contingent of Swansea fans. A couple of times towards the end of the contest, our fans were ready to spill onto the pitch in celebration. Their captain went to the referee and told him it was not safe for his players and he wanted him to stop the match. We couldn't believe the conversation he was having with the official, and a huge argument broke out in the middle of the pitch between our players and Bury's. Eventually calm returned and we won the game 1-0. News had filtered through that Southend were losing to Grimsby, hence the excitement of the fans, and when the final whistle was blown we knew we had won promotion into League One.

Three-quarters of the ground was filled with Swansea fans. The players wanted to celebrate with them and we were allowed to go into the Directors' Box to enjoy the moment. Our goalkeeper, Willy Gueret, tried to climb the steps into the box but unfortunately the police were not too supportive. Willy protested and tried to join us once again. Pushing and shoving followed and eventually Willy was arrested. A memorable day ended with us sitting in the team bus outside the police station, waiting for him to be released. Nothing came of the incident, but I have to say it was a unique way to end a promotion party.

I was able to bid farewell properly to the Vetch the following week when we played Wrexham in the final of the FAW Trophy. It was the last time Swansea City would play at the Vetch in any competition and, because we already had promotion in the bag, we were able to enjoy ourselves. It was great to play and beat a team from a higher division. In the game against Shrewsbury Town, all we had thought about as players was the need to get three points. Everything else that was going on was something of a distraction. In the Wrexham match our more relaxed attitude showed in the way we played. Although we went behind from a goal by Juan Ugarte, their prolific goal scorer, we came back to win 2-1. After scoring twice in five minutes, we never lost control of the game. When it was over, we were able to celebrate what the Vetch meant to us, and the win against Wrexham was a great way to say goodbye to the special Vetch. When I looked back on the season I had the great satisfaction of knowing I had given everything to help the club and played a big role in what was a very successful year.

The next campaign, 2005-06, was again a case of success on the field mixed with personal difficulties and struggles. Before the start of pre-season training I received a phone call from the manager, Kenny Jackett, telling me that it would probably be better if I moved on to another club. He told me that I wouldn't be playing many games, as I wasn't part of his plans for the coming season. After this devastating call, I had a long think about my next move. I was not going to be given many opportunities to play for the Swans, so should I pack my bags and go? The more I thought about the situation, the more I resolved to stay. We had just won promotion to a higher division and there would be the challenge of playing against better and tougher opposition. In addition we had moved to a wonderful stadium, and I knew that the wider pitch would suit my style of play. I reminded myself that I had worked my way back into the squad during the previous term, so I decided to stay and fight for my place.

In the early part of the season it looked like I had made the right choice. I played the first sixteen games and, at the end of that spell, we were top of League One. We played our first game at our new home with a 1-0 victory over Tranmere Rovers, and this was followed by other excellent performances, including a 7-1 thrashing of Bristol City which unfortunately cost their manager, Brian Tinnion, his job. At the end of that game I felt we had all played in a way that graced our wonderful new stadium, and I also thought our football had progressed to a new level. We were playing really well and the crowds were pouring into the Liberty Stadium. Then we were unexpectedly dumped out of the FA Cup at Stockport. For some reason, I was made the scapegoat for that defeat, and I found myself pushed onto the sidelines once again.

Our next league game was against Southend United, who were in second position, and I was not even selected in the sixteen. Towards the end of the season I was brought back for the odd game, but I didn't play often. Even when I did play, I began to feel that I probably didn't have much future at Swansea. At the end of the season, we beat Brentford in the play-off semi-final but then we lost on penalties to Barnsley in the final at the Millennium Stadium. For that match I was not in the squad and watched from the stand. Everyone was destroyed after the game, and almost all of us were in tears. Although we had come a long way from the 2002-03 season when we nearly lost our status as a

Football League club, it still hurt to get to the final and lose on penalties.

Despite struggling to get into the first team, I played in every round of the Autoglass Trophy, but was dropped for the final against Carlisle United which we won at the Millennium Stadium. I did, however, play for the last fifteen minutes, and it was a wonderful feeling to lift the trophy in front of our fans. It hurt to think that I had played in every round and yet I felt I was being singled out because the management were trying to make the point that they didn't want me for the future.

After the Barnsley match, I was out of contract. The next day I had to report to the Liberty, along with two other players whose contracts had come to an end. I was told that I was no longer required by Swansea City, and all three of us were released. It was a strange day. It didn't come as surprise as I knew Kenny Jackett didn't want me at the Liberty. In the past, when he had told me that I was not part of his plans, I had been contracted to the club, so I had the option to stay. On that day my contract had expired, so I knew I had no possibility of staying at the club and fighting my way back into the squad, as I had done in the past.

Although a few League One clubs expressed an interest in me joining their team, I decided not to sign for anyone in that league, as I did not want to play against Swansea City. I felt I owed that loyalty to the fans who had given me such wonderful support over the three seasons I had been at the club. We had done so much together. We had won two FAW trophies, won promotion from League Two, won the Autoglass Trophy, won that momentous game against Hull City and reached the play-off final. Through all those battles and triumphs, I had established a great relationship with the fans and I would have felt it was too early to sign for a club competing in the same league against Swansea City.

And so I signed for Chester City in League Two. But, before we go there together, perhaps I should explain how a young man from Catalonia ended up in the English Football League in the first place.

CHAPTER SIX

July 1973 to August 1995

Football Mad in Catalonia

I WAS BORN into a family which lived and breathed football. My father's whole life centred around his own football career. Born in Zaragoza he had played for various teams in Spain before joining his last club, Balaguer. Once his playing career came to an end he became their manager. I suppose my football career took the opposite path in that I started where my father had finished – by joining Balaguer. I started playing for my home team and then, when I was sixteen, I signed professional forms for Real Zaragoza.

One of my first memories as a child is that every Sunday I would be taken to watch my father play football. As I got older I would still watch his team, although by then he was a manager rather than a player. The mood changed, depending on the result. There was an understanding in our house that if his team won, then we would have a happy weekend. If they lost, life would be difficult. My dad was always a fierce competitor who wanted to be a winner. That attitude was there for me to see, throughout my childhood.

As well as being close to my father, I was also very attached to my mother, Amor, and my sister, Antonieta. Whenever there was an opportunity, my father and I would play games against each other. Neither of us wanted to lose, and that winning mentality, which I got from him, was a great learning process as well as being an excellent preparation for being a professional sportsman. The competition was fierce even if there was no ball involved. Cards, Ludo or any board game – it didn't matter what we played, the atmosphere would be incredibly intense, as both of us pushed for victory!

Despite his battling attitude to everything he did, he was a very pleasant man who was respectful to the winner. However, I could always tell that, behind the happy congratulatory smile, a deep hurt was hiding! It was a wonderful environment in which to grow up, but almost always the conversation was about football. Before he retired from playing at the age of forty-three, he would talk to me about the things he had to do to remain sharp enough to continue playing as a professional footballer. He exposed himself to a very strict fitness regime. Because of his commitment, I always had someone to look up to, and he was a great role model for my later quest to be a professional footballer.

From an early age, when my father became a football manager, he would chat to me about his team selections. I would jump onto his football talk and, as time went on, understand more and more. Rather than him asking me my opinion, I would ask him to explain what was happening in a game. If we were sitting together on the settee watching football on the television, we would get so absorbed in the game that it would have been possible for the whole house to burn or fall down without either of us knowing. All that mattered was our debate about the match. As far as I am concerned, if you are keen to be a professional, you can never watch enough games, managers or players. It was a great way for me to learn the trade in an environment which was warm and family orientated but, at the same time, competitive. It all gave me a great platform to understand the game in depth, and also helped me to see from an early age what I wanted to do for the rest of my life.

Sadly, I think in my later life I have reacted to results in the same way as my father. As a player and a manager, I have probably been impossible to live with if the result has gone against me. The people close to me suffer and I think you'd see that kind of difficulty in every family where someone is involved in this sport. Football is a passion which becomes a way to live. It is all about winning and, when you don't win, you feel miserable. You know that, because of the defeat, you need to find answers, and, when those answers don't come, you can't be yourself. I suppose you take for granted that at home you can be how you feel and that means the people in the same house as you will have to endure your misery. Beth, my partner, has certainly had to suffer a lot. She understands the pressure, and it is great for me to be natural in front of her. My father was exactly the same until he was able to pinpoint the reasons for things not working out in the game as he had hoped. While it is difficult for the partners or wives of footballers, I think it has to be like this. If you go home after a match that you have lost and you are happy and relaxed because the defeat hasn't affected you, then you won't last long as a professional footballer or manager.

After every game, I analyse key moments of the game where things went wrong or didn't work as well as they should. You tend not to mull over a fantastic, individual goal or a successful set piece, but you do think in depth about the disappointments. In school in Spain we used to play 'Futbol Sala' which consists of four outfield players in a small pitch, such as a five-a-side pitch. Playing in such an enclosed area means that you can grow as a player and learn technical skills. With that expertise, you can then transfer the skills to an eleven-a-side game. I think we should develop children in this way for the British game. It's a great way to develop youngsters, and allow the player to develop himself, encouraging their raw talent to shine and enjoy the game while polishing skills and increasing fitness levels. You can never play enough five-a-side football.

Youngsters are often thrown into the eleven-a-side game too early. They haven't mastered the control of the ball in tight situations. In addition, when you are playing against eleven on a big pitch, you don't get as many opportunities to touch the ball or as much time to 'live' on the ball and be comfortable with it. That's why you see Brazilians and many European players playing in that way, which shows they are happy to have the ball and do unexpected things with it. It is something which is missing from the repertoire of the young British player. The reason that the Brazilians are world beaters is that they grow up playing on the streets for six or seven hours a day. In bad conditions, which would not normally be conducive to football, they learn the art of controlling the ball and expressing themselves with it.

Since my early days of playing football, if the result has gone against me, I relax by watching football! If the final score is not important to me, then watching other teams play can be enjoyable. Football is such a great game. It is intriguing to watch other people trying to solve their football problems, instead of worrying about them. I also relax with a good meal with family and friends. Although I like music, I listen to it more in the car than at home. I can then choose the CDs to suit my mood. I like all forms of music which are easy listening. I find music a great relief and sometimes it's the best way to clear your mind.

Of course, the depression after defeat doesn't last forever. Once I have had time to recover and think through where it all went wrong, I am then ready for the next challenge. In many ways you put it all right again on the training field.

When I started playing football as a youngster I found that, having heard my father discuss and explain tactics, it helped me to understand the game as it unfolded. Football is a little like learning to drive a car. You start to understand that certain moves will result in certain consequences. If you throw a ball in the middle of twenty-two youngsters and tell them to get on with it, then, before long, some kind of pattern will develop. I was lucky in that I had been encouraged to think about what was happening and also about the best way to change things. That attitude grew out of the long chats I enjoyed with my father. He would tell me how he wanted Barcelona to play and I would share with him my views on how Real Zaragoza should play.

My father was always a very aggressive and strong player – more of a defender than anything else. Since my first game as a youngster, I was always a midfielder. I sometimes played wide midfield, but most of the time I played in the middle of the park. People who have seen us both play would probably agree that our styles were as different as day and night.

People often ask me whether my mother was interested in football. My answer to that question is, 'She had to be. She had no option!' She sacrificed a huge part of her life to accommodate the passion of her husband and son. She was very understanding and was fantastic in the way she kept the family going. Every time my father signed a contract, he knew he had to keep her happy and so he would buy her a nice present. When I was growing up in the small towns of Spain, it was a custom on the Saturday night for couples to go dancing. Of course, she was not able to go as, my father would be preparing for the match. Then, the next day, Sunday, she would have to go and watch him play, so that she would lose two days of the weekend. She was a very creative and gifted businesswoman who, as well as holding a football family together, also ran a very successful shoe shop. As a career woman she was still committed to the importance of the family, and with my father created a wonderful atmosphere at home in which my sister and I were able to enjoy our childhood. My sister graduated from university with a degree in Tourism and Business Studies.

My dad always put the family's wellbeing in front of his career. He was aware how much my mother had sacrificed to help him progress as a player. It was for this reason that he chose not to move around when he became a manager, restricting himself to managing in the region. This meant that my sister and I had a settled and solid family life without the upheaval that some footballers' children face of being uprooted every couple of years. Despite limiting himself in this way, my father still had a very professional attitude. He managed Balaguer as if he were in charge of a top team such as Barcelona. He knew that wherever you are based and whatever the team you are managing, the principles are exactly the same. From my mum and dad I was given the gift of two huge values. The first is the importance of family life which I still value and believe is important. Secondly, I inherited the wonder of football and the importance of approaching it with total commitment and professionalism.

In school I began playing five-a-side football at the age of five and then I experienced my first competitive game for Balaguer's youth team when I was nine years old. My first contact with a football came when I was two years old. My father would take me onto the pitch for a couple of hours before his game and teach me to kick the ball back and forth to him. In the primary school I was the envy of all the other boys, because my father would give me the professional balls once the club had finished with them. By the time I was nine, my football career had hit a pattern. On a Saturday I would play five-a-side for my school and then on a Sunday it would be eleven-a-side for Balaguer. I played for them at every level of youth football until I was sixteen.

Then one day at the end of a game I was approached and asked to play at Real Zaragoza in a tournament. Playing in the competition was a fantastic experience. There I was playing for a big club in Spain against the likes of Barcelona and Real Madrid. After that, Real

Zaragoza offered me a contract. While it was an exciting situation to find myself in, it was also a very hard decision to make. I was faced with the realisation that I would have to leave my warm and safe home environment to further my football career. It was very hard for my mother, but it was probably easier for my father, because he understood what the offer meant and what it could mean for my future. He gave me a lot of advice which helped me come to terms with leaving and prepared me for what lay ahead. I didn't find it too difficult leaving Balaguer as I would be only two hours away from my family. This meant that they could come and watch me play on a Sunday. So I had the best of both worlds. My family came to see me at the weekends and I had the joy of playing for a premiership side from Monday to Sunday.

The way the club is structured meant that I moved from the under-17s to under-18s, and then onto the under-19s. Thus the coaching staff work with the same block of players each year. At nineteen, if you are good enough, you progress to the B team and the next stop is the first team.

I have no recollection of the first goal I ever scored in my life. Doubtless, that would have been in school. But from those early days, I remember playing for one of the youth sides at Balaguer. It was in a huge tournament and every player in our team was under ten, but we were up against sides as old as eleven! We beat Camarasa 9-0 and I scored my first ever competitive goal. I think my most memorable strike from that time was when I scored in the tournament at Real Zaragoza. We were playing Real Madrid and, when I scored that goal, I realised that I could compete at that level. Playing in the Premiership set up at Zaragoza, I was surrounded by excellent players and I was pleased to see that I could hold my own.

Just as I remember my first goal for the club, I will also never forget my first wage packet as a professional footballer. With the money I bought my mother a fake diamond ring and my father a fake Rolex watch. Later in my career when I signed for Wigan Athletic, I bought them a real diamond ring and a real Rolex watch, and I am glad to say that they both still use them.

In 1993, when I was nineteen, I made my debut for Real Zaragoza's first team. It was their final league match, away to Atletico Madrid, and that day I felt that all the hard work had been worthwhile. The set up in Spain is very different from Britain's. Every year, out of the sixteen players in a year grouping, the club lose five, leaving eleven to progress to the next stage. There is a huge filter system every year until reaching the B Team where the standards are extremely high.

To get into the first team and play in La Liga is another step up again. The night before my first appearance for Real Zaragoza at Atletico Madrid, I will never forget the huge media attention in the hotel. I was suddenly in the presence of players I had watched throughout my childhood and was being interviewed by reporters from newspapers I had grown up reading. I was playing with players I had always admired and, of course, I knew that the next day I would be playing against footballers I had idolised. Atletico had Manolo who was a top goal scorer, and we had Nayim on our side, who had played for Tottenham Hotspur. As a child, I had collected football stamps of star players in Spain and then put them in my scrapbook. It was incredible to now see those players walk out of the stamps and become flesh and blood in the hotel foyer. Tomorrow I knew that more of the collector's gallery would be battling against me in the stadium. Despite this sense of wonder before the game, once the whistle blew to start proceedings, it just became another game.

At that time Real Zaragoza were in mid table, but the following week they appeared in the final of what is the Spanish equivalent to the FA Cup, against Real Madrid in Valencia. Just to be a part of the squad and around that dressing room when we were competing for one of the biggest football trophies in Spain was a huge experience for me. I was really young and it was all new and exciting. I wasn't on the bench for the final, but I did travel with the team. Gus Poyet had been injured before the Atletico game, so he was rested which was why I was given the chance to play. However, he recovered and came back for the final.

The following season, 1993-94, I was heavily involved in the B team, and it turned out to be a successful season.

Having just been relegated, we fought for and gained promotion back into the higher league. The club made some new signings and did well in La Liga. Training with the first team players improved my own game.

During my time at Zaragoza, I studied physiotherapy at the university in the city. I was living in digs with other players from the club, some of whom were in the youth team and some in the B team, plus a couple of first team players. I have always believed that, while you must focus on becoming a better player, it is also important that you study something other than football. There are so many things that can come along and stop your football career. Therefore, it is important that you are trained to do something else. With all the other forces and circumstances that can affect your future as a footballer, I have always believed that only forty per cent of your future is in your hands. I was very fortunate to get good A level results in school, and, when I enrolled in university, I was clear from the outset that I wanted to study a subject which was related to football. The subject gave me a good insight into the different types of injury footballers can sustain.

The game of football is not a natural pursuit. We were not born to spend every day kicking and heading heavy balls. We were born to walk and run. In the modern game, you are called upon to push your body to absolute extremes. Every day you are kicking or going into tackles about five hundred times. It is therefore vital that you learn to strengthen the muscles and the joints. It is very rare for a footballer not to come out of the profession after ten or fifteen years without some kind of physical difficulty. I suppose that is the price you are prepared to pay, but studying physiotherapy definitely helped me to prepare for the onslaughts my body would endure.

It also taught me the best way to try to prevent injuries and the various treatments available. As a player it helped me to understand my body and the best way to keep it in top condition. Now I am a manager, it helps me to understand the injuries the players endure. We are very fortunate to have a first class physiotherapist at Swansea in Richard Evans.

Zaragoza University had an excellent reputation throughout Spain and the entrance requirements were high. I achieved the marks they stipulated and I was pleased to combine my football with studies. I was at the university for three years, poring over books and working in the university as a trainee. It was also hard linking this intensive study with the demanding training schedules at the football club. I used the two very different experiences to give me a balance in my life. When I had a bad time on the training ground or in a match I would concentrate on my course and enjoy the stimulus of academic work. In the same way, if I had a bad time in the examination room, I would look forward to getting rid of all my tension and anxiety on the football pitch.

There were times when it was hard to go home to the digs at night after a challenging day at the university. In the house there were many youngsters who had no studying to do and they would often try and entice me from my books with a whole variety of distractions. In such circumstances, it was hard to study and push myself on to gain a degree. The university were extremely helpful as they knew I was playing for Real Zaragoza. They would often change the times of examinations to fit in with matches or training schedules. Sometimes I would have one-on-one exams with the teacher! It was a little scary, but it all worked out in the end.

When I left home to join Zaragoza, my father had warned me of two dangers that could wreck my future. He pointed out that just because I had signed a contract with a Spanish Premiership club, it didn't mean that I had arrived. If I had that attitude, I would sacrifice my academic studies and would probably go for the easy route of enjoying life and start drinking, instead of concentrating on keeping fit. I promised him that I would stay committed to my studies and would not drink. I actually kept both those promises. Keeping them helped me fulfil the two ambitions I had in school, which were to gain a degree and play football in La Liga. Each challenge helped me tackle the other.

The modern day professional footballer has a lot of free time on his hands, and I think it is vital that he fills it with academic studies which will prepare him for a future once his playing career is over. When I moved to Swansea City as the manager, I was glad to see that the club were working hard with the PFA and FAW, to encourage young players to study and train for another occupation. With these organisations working in conjunction with Swansea City Football Club and Neath and Port Talbot College, we are able to offer our young players tuition. The good thing about the scheme is that the college tutors come to the players and help them finish their school studies or embark on a new course of training. We now have a set up where, if a youngster joins Swansea City and wants to play for the first team and study for a degree, then we can help him in both ambitions. Mercifully, the days are now long behind us where, if you were choosing a career in football, that was your only concentration and so you had time to go to the bookies, the chippy and the pub!

At the end of season 1993-94, I was called up to do military service. In Spain, you can either join the military and train for the army or you can be given a dispensation to work within the community. I was very lucky that the council in Balaguer offered me the chance of working with the youth in the town for the nine months which I would otherwise have had to give to military service. This service normally starts when you are eighteen, but mine was postponed until I was twenty because I was studying for a degree in physiotherapy.

I returned to Balaguer from Zaragoza and played for the first team. As part of my nine months service, I ran a football school, attached to the football club, which consisted of children from the age of five to nine years old. I arranged them into different categories, so that there were separate classes for five, six, and seven-year-olds, and the eight and nine-year-olds were placed together. The latter group played competitive games every weekend. As well as organising those matches, I was also in charge of co-ordinating the work of individual coaches who coached the different age groups.

Being in charge of the eight and nine-year-olds for their matches every Sunday was my first taste of football management. I soon learned that the parents of football playing children can be somewhat 'hands on'. In fairness, they were very supportive and respectful, but at the beginning of the season I did have to set a code of conduct and behaviour which was for them rather than the children! Before I did that, it was all a bit crazy as every one seemed to have an opinion on how things should be done. I was very open and honest with them about how we should proceed, and I think that approach worked.

When the children are that age, your main aim should not be to pick a team to win. Rather, you should be selecting the players for them to develop and enjoy the experience of playing. You also have the opportunity to try various new things, because, at that age, they are very open to tuition and suggestions on how to play. There are two things that drive the children forward. Firstly, if they are receiving good coaching then they see that they are getting better every day. Secondly, as long as the sessions are structured properly, they enjoy what they are doing. I believe those two elements will feed them with a passion for football. The children were too young for the parents to show any aggression in the games towards other players or the officials. They should have been encouraging an atmosphere of enjoyment amongst the youngsters. On the whole, this is what they did, but sometimes there was the rare occasion when the parents' passion worked against the children.

All the children with whom I worked were recruited from the primary schools in the area. Members of the club would go into the schools and then invite the best players to join the youth scheme at Balaguer Football Club. In many ways, it was an elite group within the town, but, once you got them together, I worried less about them winning and more about them discovering the passion for playing and developing into the best players they could be.

I think there is a difference between the coaching of young children in Spain and Britain. In this country there is too much emphasis on tactics and how the coaches want things to be done. Children are told to play in a certain way, and there is a danger of stifling their individuality and natural talent. In Spain the attitude is that you are looking for the raw talent and you allow the boy to express himself until he is about fifteen or sixteen. It is only then that he will be coached. Otherwise, if you coach a player from the age of five, by the time he is fifteen, he will be exactly the same player. He will not have developed naturally or in unexpected ways.

Looking at the way young players are developed in Britain, I sometimes feel that they are being created by a coaching kit. The result is often that we are producing the same player around all the clubs. In the past, young players were taught by British coaches to clear their lines and try to play percentage football. They are not given that advice abroad. If they are in their own penalty area with the ball, they are more likely to be encouraged to play their way out of trouble and express their natural talent. The development of the player's own ability is seen as more important than the result.

Looking back on my time with the football school at Balaguer, I am encouraged by the fact that three of the youngsters with whom I worked have made it in the professional game in Spain. Even those who have not made it to the Balaguer First Team remember those times with fondness. Not everyone can make it as a professional footballer, but I hope that all those boys I taught will keep a passion for football throughout their lives.

I would never have got on the ladder to a career in

professional football with out the support of my family. When I was nineteen and playing in the B team for Real Zaragoza, the league we were in covered the whole of Spain. This sometimes meant that there would be a twelve-hour journey to play a game. My parents would make the trip to watch me play. They did not miss one of my matches that season. It must have cost them a fortune. That support meant so much to me. When I played in Britain, they came over three or four times a year to watch me, and now I am manager, they come over regularly to watch the Swans.

I speak to my parents every day on the phone and I consider it money well spent. They are both retired, but my father now watches my nephew, Pau, every week, who is playing for Balaguer. My sister also follows my career. She played football and basketball and, after gaining a degree, she now works for the Balaguer Town Council as the Events Director.

At the beginning of 1995-96 season, I was told that Dave Whelan, chairman of Wigan Athletic, was interested in signing me. At that time tourists came to Spain from Britain, but it was very unusual for players to leave Spain and play in Britain. Along with Jesus Seba and Isidro Diaz, I signed for the Lancashire club and we three players became known as The Three Amigos. We took advantage of the new Bosman ruling which gave footballers the freedom to move around Europe. As well as being a turning point in my life I think our move acted as an opening to many Spanish players. It opened their eyes to the excellent structure of the English League and the many opportunities there were to play there.

CHAPTER SEVEN

August 1995 to July 2001

The Three Amigos

ROM ZARAGOZA TO WIGAN. I don't think many people had made that journey before, but it was one I made at the start of the 1995-96 season. Many players do what other players have done and they spend their lives treading in other people's footprints.

I look at famous players such as Johann Cruyff. He was unique in that, as a player and a manager, he didn't follow others. He did everything in his own way. I have always been attracted by that spirit and attitude. For myself I never want to do what others have done or tread the safe ground; I always want a challenge to face. Because of this view, I have never been in a position where I think my life has to follow a certain pattern. That openness to life developing in whatever way it wants means that I will always be ready for the next test.

Jesus, Isidro and I were three young lads who all dreamed about playing regularly in La Liga, and then, suddenly, we were all invited to play in the British game.

It was a game we knew about through watching the likes of Liverpool, Manchester United and Arsenal on television, but we hadn't really heard of Wigan. The approach came as something of a shock, but, despite that fact, it was certainly very interesting. I always felt that Dave Whelan was one step ahead of us. He invited us to visit Wigan for a week and encouraged us to look around before deciding whether we liked the area and the set up at the club.

The day we landed in Britain we had that feeling that we wanted to sign. Dave Whelan was an extremely successful businessman and entrepreneur, and we wanted to be part of what he had in his mind. He came across as a person who would turn everything he touched to gold. He had certainly done that with the one sports shop he bought with the money he was given after the serious injury he sustained in the 1960 FA Cup Final. That one shop eventually became two and so on until JJB Sports became a multi-million pound business operating in Britain and throughout Europe.

On the day he talked with us, Wigan Athletic were a Third Division side, which was the bottom tier of the Football League. Yet now, as I write thirteen years later, everything he said he wanted to achieve has been done with Wigan, a Premiership team. That success is all the more remarkable when you remember that they only entered the Football League from non-league football in 1978. He is a person who never changes his ideas or vision. He is a very determined and focused individual. There are not all that many people like Dave Whelan in football or life in general.

We came over in July 1995 and, as well as being accompanied by our agent, we always had someone with us from JJB Sports who could speak Spanish. Everyone who dealt with us that week made us feel special and welcome. They even organised a trip to Blackpool and, somehow, our visit was made on a sunny day! We were lured into thinking that the weather in Britain was all right. We even told our friends and families on our mobiles that it was not very different from Spain!

Dave Whelan went out of his way to make us feel that he wanted us to sign for the club. In football as in everything else in life, it is important to feel that you are wanted. Springfield Park was a wonderful ground with a terrific history attached to it. In many ways, it was similar to the Vetch – compact and with a great atmosphere. But even at that stage he had plans for the new ground which he showed us. He took us into his office and shared his ambitions with us. He was determined to get Wigan into the Premiership. Although at that stage they were in the bottom division, he was full of hope. He told us there was not much difference between Division Three and Division Two. 'Once we get there,' he said, 'we will get into Division One. That will be a big gap. But once we're there it is just one section away from the Premiership.' Already he is one step ahead of us and is now selling us a Third Division club which is in the Premiership! He had such an infectious vision; you wanted to be part of it. By the end of the week we had all swallowed the Whelan dream and signed for Wigan Athletic.

Four years after joining the Latics, the new JJB stadium was opened and the first match was a friendly against Manchester United. Then, of course, we were two divisions below the Red Devils, and it is amazing to think that nine years later in the final match of the Premiership 2007-08 season, the same fixture was to decide the destination of the Premiership title. Wigan, which had come out of non-league and was in the bottom division when I joined them, was now giving the Champions of Europe and the Premiership champions a great fight and something of a fright. It just goes to show that Dave Whelan got what he wanted. That day during the friendly, he must have been thinking 'I want to compete in an official match against Manchester United.' At the end of 2007-08, Manchester United needed three points against Wigan to be crowned champions of the Premiership.

When Dave Whelan talked to us, he told us he wanted to be in the Premiership within five years. It took him nine, but he got there! The arrival of three Spanish players in Wigan caused quite a stir in the area as well as in the world of football. Only Nayim had made the journey before us, leaving Spain to play for Tottenham Hotspur.

The view throughout Britain among football fans was that the Spanish players would be fine in the summer, but that they would probably go into hiding when the rain and the British winter arrived! Many also felt that they would not be consistent in their performances, as it would be impossible to play the way they had been trained in the lower leagues. In reality I suppose there had always been that football debate between the two different styles of play. It was, therefore, a great challenge for us, The Three Amigos. I have absolutely wonderful memories of my time at Wigan Athletic.

Graham Barrow was the manager, and it must have been a huge issue for him. He had to handle the problem of having two diametrically opposed approaches to football in the one team. Despite the potential difficulties, all the players gelled well together. Jesus Seba and Isidro Diaz were both wide players. They were fantastically gifted players who liked to slow the game down, have one-on-one battles and score goals! I played in the centre of midfield and it was my role to play as the link-up and try to get the ball to the front men. It worked very well as we were fairly successful in our home matches at Springfield Park. Unfortunately, it was a different story away from home, and we found it difficult to maintain that level of performance.

It was a difficult time to be a manager of Wigan Athletic, because the expectations of the fans were very demanding. In addition to the fans, Dave Whelan also had huge ambitions which he wanted fulfilled. As far as he was concerned he wanted quick results and wanted to see the club move forward speedily. In the five seasons I was at Wigan, I served under nine different managers. In many ways it was a shame that we didn't have time to develop as a team, as the pressure was always on us to win at all costs. In my first season at Springfield Park, 1995-06, Graham Barrow was sacked. His dismissal followed a home defeat at the hands of Mansfield which we lost 6-2. Graham Barrow was replaced by Frank Lord as caretaker manager and, under his leadership, it was the first time that all three Spanish players played together. Under Graham, this had not happened as we were all still trying to adapt to the British game and the way Wigan played. Frank Lord was soon replaced by John Deehan, and, at the end of his first season in charge, we were on the brink of the play-offs on the last Saturday of the season. We had to beat Northampton Town to secure a play-off position. Northampton had no chance of promotion but were in no danger of relegation. Although they were safe and had nothing to play for, they made life difficult for us and the game ended in a draw, which meant that we missed out on promotion. We had just narrowly missed out on promotion, which was some achievement when you consider that the previous year, when Dave Whelan and Graham Barrow moved to the club, Wigan were rock bottom. Whelan's aim in that first season was to survive and then to win promotion in the next. Of course, we didn't achieve that, but just missing out on the play-offs meant that the club was making good progress.

In football there is a saying that when the expectations are high you always want more. Despite these feelings of disappointment throughout the club and among the fans, I was pleased with my performances at the end of that first campaign. I was the top scorer with 13 league goals and that season I thoroughly enjoyed my football. I was given a free role to play and I ended up with the honour of being named in the PFA Team of the Year. I also won the Player of the Year Award at the club, an award which was made as a result of the votes of the fans. It all meant that 1995-96 was for me a memorable year and a good introduction to the British game.

Although all three of us settled fairly quickly into our new lives in Wigan, I think Jesus Seba found it the most difficult. He had played for Spain under-21s and had made a huge number of appearances for Real Zaragoza in the top league, and yet he wasn't used as regularly as Isidro and I were. We all three faced a big battle in adapting to a new style of coaching and a new approach to football. To cope with the massive changes we were facing we felt it was important to approach our football lifestyle in the same way as we had in Spain. It meant that, once we had finished training for the day at Springfield Park, we would go home and have our siesta. And then we would be ready to go out again, this time to hunt proper food such as pasta dishes. We would normally hit the town at 5pm, only to find that in the winter it would be dark and throughout the year at that time of day the shops, cafes and restaurants would be closed. We slowly began to realise that we were out of harmony with the way everyone else was living in the country. It was quite a challenge for us to find places that would feed our Spanish lifestyles.

Eventually, in Wigan, we found an Italian restaurant called Milano's, run by a Spanish person called Ramon, who had been living and working in the Manchester area for many years. He looked after us extremely well and allowed us to go there for lunch and dinner. In many ways he fitted around our training timetable and our siesta times! We couldn't accommodate the opening times of the shops, because we were either training or sleeping. When I look back to 1995 and compare the situation with today, it is now completely different. In those days after five o'clock you couldn't get anything, whereas nowadays most places are open throughout the day and evening.

There are many flash and wealthy people living in the centre of modern day Manchester and the city is now full of continental restaurants and wine bars. In 1995 we couldn't even find an espresso, so it was very difficult if you wanted to have a coffee and play a game of cards, as is the custom in Spain. The town of Wigan, although small, is very attractive with some fine buildings, and the people are open and friendly. In spite of this, the cultural differences were so enormous that we felt we were going against the stream. It was good that three of us had moved there together, because I think if any of us had been there on our own it would have been Mission Impossible.

Because we were in the situation together, we were able to talk and laugh about it, realise that we were culture-shocked, and select the positives out of what was happening. One of the positives was that our favourite Spanish radio programme, which kept us informed about what was going on in the Sports world back home, started an hour earlier because of the time difference between the countries. In Spain it started at midnight and went on for two hours. In Wigan, with the help of satellite, we could listen at 11pm, go to bed at one o'clock in the morning and still have eight hours sleep before reporting for training in the morning.

With the help of Jesus and Isidro, with Ramon creating a little slice of Spain in the middle of Wigan, and with the friendship and support of everyone from the town and those connected with the club, I was able to acclimatise and I thoroughly enjoyed everything I did. It is strange to think that two restaurant owners have played a large part in the success of my career. The owner of El Paco in Swansea saved the club from extinction and I believe that Ramon in Wigan helped to keep The Three Amigos on British soil. I also have to say that the club made me feel wanted and accepted, from Dave Whelan to the youngest fan.

Not only did I face the challenge of adapting to a new culture, but there was also the problem of the differences in approaches to playing the game. Geographically, it is a long way from Real Zaragoza to Wigan Athletic. It is also a huge journey in terms of football philosophy. The major contrast for me was that on the continent it is drummed into you that if you want to make it as a professional footballer you have to look after yourself, so that you can compete against the other members in the squad. You also learn the importance of eight hours sleep, the need to cut out alcohol and to eat the right kind of food. All of a sudden, I found myself in a footballing atmosphere where the philosophy seemed to be that as long as you give everything, everything is allowed. It was a great shock for me to realise what the famous British team bonding sessions actually involved! Remarkably, the next morning the players would be on the training field. It reminded me of the phrase, 'If you are good enough to party, you need to be good enough to work.'

In Spain, players would not go out for a meal with other players the night before a training session. They would know that their bodies would not be up to the demands of a thorough workout if they had been filling it with food and drink the night before. Seeing this completely different attitude to football widened my ideas and options. It made me aware that at the end of the day one's approach to preparing for football matches is a matter of opinion. It was a great learning experience for me to see that, as a player and subsequently a manager, I would have to select the approach which suited me best.

During my second season at Wigan, 1996-97, we won the League Two Championship (then called Division 3). In the brief time I had been there, I had seen a huge transformation. From a club on the brink of relegation to the Conference to one which had just missed out on promotion in my first season, we were now the undisputed champions going up into the equivalent of League One (Division 2). Some of the football we played that season, especially at home, was absolutely fantastic. The playing surface was first class and the fans really got behind us in all the games and enjoyed the season as much as the players. The groundsman Dave Pinch won the 'Groundsman of the Year' award, and it was as important to the club as any other trophy. Having such a good pitch helped us in the way we wanted to play.

John Deehan had made some fine signings in the close season and assembled a good squad. Because of the way Isidro and I liked to play on the ball, I think John Deehan saw that the team would have to be stronger at the back and he realised the team needed to close the back door more than they had in the previous season. Colin Greenall returned to the club and he also signed Gavin Johnson, both of whom were strong in defence. Pat McGiven, a good old-fashioned centre half, was signed on loan from Manchester United, and the loan was later made a permanent move.

Previous page: *last football campaign played at the Vetch Field.*

Below: *scoring against Nottingham Forest at the Liberty, 2005/06 season.*

Opposite, above: *before kick off versus Cambridge United in the last season at the Vetch.*

Opposite, below: *first ever League game at the Liberty Stadium.*

Against Kidderminster in our promotion campaign in League One.

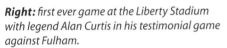

January 2006: versus MK Dons and Bristol City.

Right: *first ever game at the Liberty Stadium with legend Alan Curtis in his testimonial game against Fulham.*

Below: against Colchester at the Liberty, December 2005.

Top left: *versus Chester at the Deva Stadium.*

Below: *at Saltergate with our fans after the last League game of the 2005/06 season.*

Above: winning the Football League trophy at the Millenium Stadium.

Below: FAW Cup, after the final at the Racecourse

First campaign at the new home of the Swans.

Extending deal as Manager of Swansea City with Chairman Huw Jenkins.

Kicking every ball – from the touchline.

Winning the Coca Cola Manager of the Month.

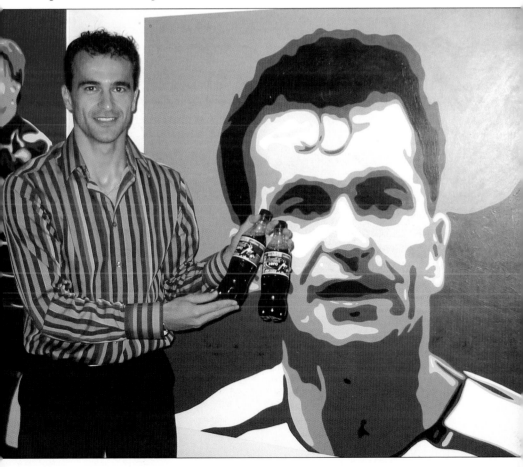

Receiving the LMA League One Manager of the Year 2008 from England Manager, Fabio Capello.

Swansea City Open Bus parade, as Champions.

We had a good mix of youth and experience, with proven strikers such as David Lowe and Graeme Jones, who is now my assistant at the Liberty Stadium. In that season Graeme was the top scorer with 33 goals, a fact which he has insisted on telling everyone ever since, and also something I feel I have to mention. Throughout the campaign, we were neck and neck with Fulham, who were recently funded by Al Fayed's money. The championship went down to the final day of the season and, in the end, we won the title on goal difference.

We secured promotion in a Tuesday night fixture at home against Colchester United. When I moved to play in England, I had been told many times: 'If you are playing a southern team at Springfield Park on a Tuesday night, you won't have to worry about the result. After that long journey up and the prospect of the same after the game, the Southerners will not be up for it.' I always found that a difficult idea to accept, because I often wondered what possible difference it could make to professional footballers. It was certainly not an easy passage for us on that particular Tuesday night. Colchester United pushed us all the way and we won a hard fought game 1-0, with Pat McGiven scoring from a corner. It was my first taste of winning a British football trophy and it was a wonderful feeling, one which all the players, club officials and fans shared. Although it had taken us over two full seasons to secure promotion since Dave Whelan had bought the club, we felt that what we had achieved was huge and we were now heading in the right direction. In addition to the club's triumphs it was another great season for me personally, as I got into the PFA Team of the Year for the second successive year.

The end of that memorable season also marked the end of the contracts for The Three Amigos, as we had all just signed for two years. By the time our contracts expired, Jesus had already left, as he wasn't getting as many minutes on the field as he had hoped. He was missing many aspects of Spanish life and had found it difficult to settle in Britain. It was a good move for him, as he joined Real Zaragoza and ended up playing for them in La Liga. He experienced the harsh irony of football in that he couldn't get into a team playing in the old Third Division of the British system and yet found a regular place in a top Spanish side. Isidro and I re-signed for the team and played many of games in the 1997-98 season.

In the close season I had approaches from a few clubs including one from a club in La Liga in Spain. I had to make the decision whether I wanted to go back to Spain, as Jesus Seba had done, or whether I wanted to stay in Wigan. As I thought the situation and the options through it became clear to me that, in football, it is all about the immediate challenge in front of you, rather than trying to go as high as you can in the game. So, in the end it was not a difficult decision to commit myself to Wigan. Because of the way Wigan had welcomed and treated me, I felt very attached to the club, and therefore I wanted to be loyal to them. That is why I was happy to sign a new four-year contract.

As the new boys in League One, we found it a totally different challenge and it took us a little while to adapt. Although capable of beating anyone on our day, we struggled to find our feet, and it has to be admitted it was a very up and down season. We certainly didn't play with the consistency you need if you are going to achieve promotion, but we did finish on a high with a flourish of good results, securing a mid-table position just outside the play-offs.

When I first arrived at Springfield Park, the fan base was fairly small, with gates between four and five thousand. I was aware that there were two professional clubs in the town, with the famous Rugby League club just down the road. I honestly thought that this would help the cause of sport in the town and wrongly assumed that the inhabitants would support both the rugby and football teams. My assumption couldn't have been further from the truth as there was a real love-hate relationship between the two sets of fans. If you supported the rugby team, you wouldn't admit to following the Latics, and, of course, the opposite was also true. Slowly though, I began to see the groups moving together, and, as the team became more successful, the crowds got bigger and the gates started moving towards the ten thousand mark.

Wigan itself is situated in a densely-populated area with six million people living within a twenty-five mile radius. Of course, with Manchester United, Manchester City, Blackburn Rovers and Bolton Wanderers all situated in that area, there were lots of other attractions for the football fan, but I still believed that if you played good football you would attract big crowds. I think Dave Whelan was aware of that and wanted to see the fan base increase. At the time I was there it was growing all the time. When the three of us arrived, we saw how strong and committed the football fans were. They had seen the club progress from non-league into the Football League, and, as followers of football, they were in the minority compared with those following rugby. This gave them a fanaticism and a family-type loyalty, both of which stayed throughout the rise of the club into the Premiership. The fans gave us Three Amigos a terrific welcome, and added to the sense of fun by coming to the matches wearing sombreros. That core of passionate fans got behind the football club and pushed them into the top flight.

The following three seasons saw Wigan develop as a strong League One side, but, although we became a much better team, we were unfortunate enough to reach the play- offs in three successive seasons yet just miss out every time. In the 1998-99 we lost to Manchester City in the semi-finals and the following year we progressed to the final after defeating Millwall. At Wembley we played

Gillingham and, although we were beating them 2-1, we finally lost 3-2. The following season, 2000-01, we endured more heartbreak. Having drawn 0-0 against Reading in the semi-final, we went to the Madejski Stadium for the second leg. With five minutes to go we were 1-0 up and heading for our second consecutive Wembley appearance when disaster struck. We conceded two goals before the final whistle, so Reading progressed to meet Walsall, who beat them and progressed to the Championship.

After the Wembley final, my contract expired and Steve Bruce, the new manager who had taken over from Bruce Rioch, spoke to all the players whose contracts were up. After that meeting I genuinely thought that I would receive a new contract. Unfortunately, although he had only been at the JJB Stadium for a couple of months, he left the club and became the manager at Crystal Palace. This left me in a state of limbo without a contract. I had to move on.

I received offers from other clubs in League One, but having been made to feel so at home by the Wigan fans I felt it would have been disloyal to play for another team in the same league. That was a big factor in my decision to accept the offer to play in the SPL for Motherwell. So, after acclimatising to the English culture and weather, I now prepared for somewhere that would be even colder and rainier than Wigan. It was over the border for me!

CHAPTER EIGHT

July 2001 to August 2002

The Motherwell of all Disasters

I FOUND the whole idea of playing in the Scottish Premier League very attractive. I was excited at the prospect of playing against Rangers and Celtic, both of whom play to crowds in excess of 50,000 and compete at Champions League level. I knew it was going to be a different sort of challenge from the English league, and was also pleased at the thought of working with Billy Davies, the manager. Billy was an extremely enthusiastic person, who had made seven new signings in the close season. He was determined to make the club the third force in Scotland, behind Rangers and Celtic.

I was excited at the prospect of working with someone as dynamic and open minded as Billy Davies and he had taken the club forward in the previous season, so much so, that they had just missed out on a European spot.

There was a buzz around the club that we could build

on the promise of Billy's work. But in football, continuity is a big thing and was something we didn't have in the dressing room during the close season. Important players with huge roles within the squad left the club, including Andy Goram, Don Goodman and John Spencer which meant new players had to come in. There were as many as seven new players coming to Fir Park, which in football terms means a lot of work and time to settle and gel together into a successful formula.

I had been at the club for a whole month before I met the chairman. John Boyle was very different from Dave Whelan, who had been a large presence and driving force behind everything that went on at Wigan. John Boyle seemed to distance himself from what was going on at the club.

There was, however, optimism when I joined the club, especially as Billy Davies had been so busy in the transfer market. With players like Mark Brown from Rangers, Carl Reddy from QPR, Steve Cosgrove from Manchester United, Andy Dow from Aberdeen and David Kelly from Sheffield United signing for the club, hopes were high that The Well would have a good season. We also had an exciting group of youngsters with the likes of Stephen Pearson, Keith Lasley, Dougie Ramsay and James McFadden, who all had great potential, hunger and football ability.

Sadly, the reality was very different. There was no time for Billy to work with a new project and give direction to the new partnerships on the pitch. A lack of common sense surrounded the whole situation which meant that we had to get a result in the next game to keep Billy Davies in charge. That game was Rangers at Ibrox and after a more than expected defeat Billy Davies' time was up, which led to sadness in the dressing room. I was surprised he wasn't given longer to try and turn things around. He was replaced by Eric Black, with Terry Butcher, the ex-Ipswich and England international, as his assistant. Eric Black set about trying to change things quickly and bought new players, including Eric Deloumeaux from French second division side Le Havre. The three other players to join the club were Yon Soloy, David Ferrere and Francois Dubordeau.

We continued to struggle throughout the season, with relegation to Division One looking a distinct possibility. Unfortunately the aim of the season had become one of avoiding relegation in a clear two-horse race between St Johnstone and ourselves. As you can imagine every ninety minutes had huge significance and brought huge pressure. Our victory away to St Johnstone at the end of March 2002 suggested we were going to be safe and that was confirmed when we took a point from the same club in April. One of the ironies about the battle against St Johnstone was that Graeme Jones, who had been with me at Wigan, where we had tried to win games together, was now playing against me. Because of my friendship with Graeme I was sad when I saw the Saints relegated to the First Division. I have always had a strong footballing relationship with Graeme and a high respect for his ability to understand the game, despite the fact that our footballing backgrounds could not be further apart. With his discipline, organisational skills and his shared philosophy for the game I was delighted to bring him from Hamilton Academicals to the Liberty Stadium as my assistant manager.

Sadly, that April was to become memorable not for staying in the SPL but because John Boyle put the club into administration with just two games remaining. The worst experience I encountered in my footballing life came the next day when the administrator walked into the football club and terminated players' contracts, plus those of other staff at the club. There were nearly twenty people made redundant with no protection. It is hard to explain what the feelings were around the place after such a bombshell. It is great to know that this situation can never happen in any of the clubs in the Football League, where players' contracts are well protected and other routes are pursued to find solutions for everyone affected.

This put the club in a very difficult situation. As well as all the problems caused to every player's family there was the bigger danger of the club getting relegated and its future blighted. Looking back, I am sure that every player or staff and office member who was involved in that situation has come out of it stronger, and learned from it. But the bigger worry was the future of Motherwell Football Club and its fans, as the whole fiasco could have destroyed a huge footballing tradition and institution. As it was, Motherwell Football Club had to survive some very difficult times, but the fans were not too heavily punished as, although they finished bottom of the league the following season, they didn't get relegated.

Putting the club into administration meant it could continue to trade, and we were allowed to fulfil our fixtures. In the English leagues, clubs who have gone into administration, such as Bournemouth, Rotherham United, Leeds United, Luton Town and Wrexham, have had at least ten points deducted. Such a penalty was not in operation in the Scottish League, and I was glad for the fans that they did not have to suffer the horror of their team being demoted into Division One. The Motherwell fans are fanatical and they showed their dedication to the club with their terrific support during the first game we played after John Boyle's announcement, away to Kilmarnock, cheering us on to a 4-1 victory.

Our financial situation was dire and everyone had an opinion on why it had happened. Despite the number of views held by people associated with the club, the players had not had any idea of what was going on behind the scenes. It all came as a great shock to us.

Pat Nevin, the ex-Everton and Scotland international who was the club's chief executive, did not think that Boyle had taken the right course of action. He believed that if more cash had been injected into the club, Motherwell would have turned the corner and they would be able to compete once again to become the number three club in Scotland. That view was shared by Eric Black, the manager, and they both resigned from their posts, agreeing to help the administrators as much as they could. Pat Nevin formed a consortium with the aim of buying the club, but he was unable to raise the necessary finances. After stepping down as manager, Eric Black was replaced by Terry Butcher for the last couple of games.

Although they mustered up all the support they could, the fans were devastated by the situation. In Scotland, if you follow a team other than Rangers or Celtic, then I think you must be passionate about that club. The town of Motherwell is just fifteen minutes away from Glasgow where Celtic and Rangers play, yet between six and eight thousand people would turn out to see us every week. Despite the gloom and despair which had settled on Fir Park, the fans rallied to do all they could to help Motherwell Football Club survive financially. Working closely with the club, they formed a joint initiative called 'Well Worth Saving'. The main idea was to get the fans to turn out in force for a specially arranged match against the Italian Serie A side, Chievo, and for the final home league game against Dundee.

While affecting the supporters, the players were also disturbed by what had happened. I had played only one year of a three-year contract. I and the other contracted players, including all seven who had been signed by Billy Davies, were made redundant. Those whose contracts had finished were released. We were all in the same boat, having to find a new club on our own. Going into administration affected the players, because many at Motherwell had moved their families up to Scotland. In football, there is security with a three-year contract, as you feel you can concentrate on your game for that period of time and not worry about your family or other domestic and financial issues. When something like this occurs, you lose all sense of safety and feel incredibly unprotected. The set up in Scotland is not as strict as in England. The English Professional Footballers' Association would never allow clubs to terminate the contracts of players. At Motherwell, however, nine of us were made redundant and another ten released without having the protection which a contract should bring.

Playing at a club that was sinking fast into financial disarray did have the advantage for me in that it brought a maturity to my playing and my attitude to the sport. It is a huge challenge to play week in and week out when the storm clouds are gathering over the club and you feel you have little support from upstairs. In such situations, it is up to the players to try to salvage something for themselves and the fans. Under such pressure, I believe we gelled as a team and there were some very strong friendships made.

Possibly one of my closest friends at Motherwell was

the striker David 'Ned' Kelly. Ned was famous for many things, but especially the fact that, although he was born in Birmingham, he had chosen to play for the Republic of Ireland, with whom he was involved in two World Cups. He always liked to remind everyone that he had scored Ireland's only goal in the game against England in 1995. Billy Davies signed Ned from Sheffield United and their relationship was carried on once they had both left Motherwell as Ned became Billy's assistant manager, first at Preston North End and then at Derby County.

Ned and I would spend hours talking about football and discussing tactics. I suppose it is not surprising that both of us ended up in football management. When we were not sorting out every team in Scotland, England or the rest of the world, we would play the game Spoof, where each player has to guess how many coins the other is holding in their hand, from none to three. The game could go on forever, sometimes ending in the 'best of hundreds', rather than the best of three! Whoever lost had to buy the other a meal and, as I was a consistent winner, I ate sumptuously and often at the expense of Ned's credit card.

Talking of the high points of that dark year at Motherwell, I have saved the best until last. For the first seven weeks of my time in Scotland I stayed in the charming Moorings Hotel. The staff were friendly, helpful and incredibly supportive of a Spanish footballer finding his way in Scotland. It was claimed that the hotel was haunted, but

I very quickly became haunted by a vision of beauty who was doing her work experience there. Beth was studying at Strathclyde University and her time at the hotel was part of her marketing and tourism degree. Without sounding too much like a character from a romantic Hollywood film, you just know when you meet the woman of your dreams. We have been together ever since, and Beth is a fantastic support and special person, putting up with the many hours when I am away on football duties.

Having just settled in Scotland and having found someone who made all the difficulties of Motherwell Football Club tolerable, I was on my way again, this time down to the Midlands to play for the Championship club Walsall.

CHAPTER NINE

August 2002 to January 2003

Going in all Directions

A FTER MOTHERWELL, I signed for manager Colin Lee, who was in charge of Championship side Walsall. As a player he had shot to fame in 1977, scoring four goals on his début for Tottenham Hotspur in their 9-0 victory over Bristol Rovers in the old Second Division. For many years he had been assistant to Mark McGhee at Reading, Leicester and Wolves. In January 2002 he was appointed manager at Walsall, and staved off relegation into League One by steering the team to the safety of eighteenth position.

Although I was only there for a brief period, it was an interesting experience. Closely surrounded by the big clubs of Wolverhampton Wanderers, Birmingham City, West Bromwich Albion and Aston Villa, Walsall was certainly regarded in the football world as a club which had to work hard to attract new players and maintain a strong fan base. The club had to find a different recipe to enable it to compete against such powerful clubs in the division and in the locality. Their success was due to their excellent scouting policy.

Knowing that they could not compete in the British transfer market, they had scoured the leagues abroad for players they could attract to the Midlands. For me, it was a wonderful experience to sit in a dressing room where so many different cultures came together to fight for the success of Walsall. The squad consisted of three Spaniards, one Portuguese, one Brazilian, one New Zealander and two Australians. It was great playing with so many individuals who had different influences on their game and allowed those influences to show in the way they played.

Of course, I wasn't at Walsall very long, because in the following February Brian Flynn asked me to sign for Swansea City, to help fight off the threat of relegation into the Conference. I have already described that battle and the details of the subsequent seasons before my contract ran out and I moved to Chester City in League Two.

When I think about my times at Walsall and Chester City there is an extraordinary coincidence. I joined Walsall in July 2002 and left them in February 2003 because Swansea City wanted me to join them as a player. I signed for the Cestrians in July 2006, and left in February 2007, again because Swansea City had asked me to join them, although this time as manager. And people say that there is no rhyme or reason to the game of football!

Chester City is a cosy club in a fairly small city, who have to fight for their own identity. Their situation is similar to that of Walsall in that they are surrounded by bigger clubs within a few miles radius. Manchester United, Manchester City, Everton and Liverpool are all just forty-five minutes' drive away. It is very difficult for them to attract large crowds, and their average attendance is normally in the region of two-and-a-half to three thousand. They are a family club with a very committed fan base. The fans who choose to support Chester City, instead of the other glamorous names within a one hour drive, show their passion and loyalty towards the club. Their warmth and voice makes Chester City a great place for the players to enjoy their football. Honours have not come their way very often, and, apart from a couple of promotions into the third tier of football, the current League One, the fans have had little to shout about except for a wonderful run in the League Cup in 1975 when they were narrowly defeated by Aston Villa in the semi- final.

My main reason for moving to Chester was to be reunited with Graham Barrow, the assistant manager, and to work with the manager, Mark Wright. I first met Graham Barrow in June 1995 in Spain when he was at the helm of Wigan Athletic. I always admired his professionalism which had been demonstrated to me in the summer of 1995, when he had flown over to Barcelona and driven for nearly two hours into the middle of nowhere to watch a cup

game to assess two potential Wigan players, Isidro Diaz
and myself. After giving a positive report on both of us, he
also enquired about the number six player on the opposing
team, Las Palmas. He was a silky playmaker, quite slim,
but Graham believed that as a young player he had some
potential. Las Palmas prevented Graham's enquiry from
progressing any further, but that number six turned out
to be Juan Carlos Valeron, who went on to accumulate
over £15 million in transfer fees, enjoying hero status with
Atletico Madrid, Las Palmas and Deportivo La Coruna, as
well as carving out an international career of well over 45
caps with Spain. Not bad scouting!

I was extremely impressed with the way Wigan Athletic
worked and the professionalism and determination that
Graham Barrow showed. I couldn't wait to join him for
an adventure in the British game with Wigan Athletic.
Graham has got a great knowledge of the game and sets
extremely high standards in everything he does. He was
a leader as a player and he took that into his managerial
career. He is very demanding with a great manner and
impressive man-management skills. He made sure that
we, the three Spanish boys he took to Wigan Athletic,
settled in quickly so we could enjoy our football. Over
and above ensuring that we settled into the football club,
he also welcomed us as part of his own family. We were
regularly invited to his home to practise our English over
dinner with his wife Mags and two children, James and

Hannah. Being so far from our own families this helped us feel at home in our new environment.

Graham was something of a hero to the Chester City fans as he had been a loyal servant of the club as a player for eight years. In the 2000-01 season, he was their manager for a season and returned as assistant to Mark Wright.

I enjoyed playing for Mark and Graham and had a good time at Chester, making 31 appearances and picking up a few Man of the Match awards. I suppose I expected to play out my days there with Graham. I thought I would play for another five or six years and then, hopefully, become a coach. Neither plan materialised as the call to manage Swansea came in February, finishing my working relationship with Graham Barrow and Mark Wright much earlier than I had anticipated.

Whilst at Walsall and Chester City, I appeared on Sky Sports' Sunday afternoon programme, *Spanish Football*. In fact I began working on it while I was at Wigan Athletic and am still involved with the programme. I have to blame, or thank, the then manager, Bruce Rioch. It all started when *Spanish Football* organised a feature to discuss the differences between the British and Spanish game over a nice Spanish meal in a central London restaurant. The views were shared between Jordi Cruyff (playing for Manchester United at the time), Albert Ferrer (from Chelsea), the journalist Guillem Balaguer and myself, and the item offered an interesting vision of two very different games observed from various angles and seen from different points of view.

After the interview, Dave Lawrence, then the show's producer, asked me whether I would consider appearing on the programme every Sunday. It would involve watching live games from La Liga and then offering expert analysis. My Wigan boss at the time was Bruce Rioch, and so I asked his opinion. Bruce was very supportive and said, 'Anything you can do in life that is football-related and doesn't interfere with your game you should do.' So, when Dave Lawrence said, 'Would you like to try?' I immediately answered, 'Yes', although I still had some worries about my spoken English. However, I realised the programmes would put me under the right kind of pressure, so I'd have to learn very quickly.

I have been doing the programmes for nine seasons now, and see it more as a joy than a job. I am thrilled to work with such professionals and people who have a passion for the Spanish game. When I started, I thought that the Italian game was second to the English game in terms of its popularity among British football fans. I am now convinced that, as a result of players such as David Beckham, Jonathan Woodgate, Steve McManaman, Vinny Samways and Michael Owen playing in Spain, the Spanish game has now replaced the Italian game as the second most popular in Britain.

It's been a great life, with so many varied and exciting influences on my footballing career. But before we end the story so far, let us take one last look at Swansea's wonderful title-winning season of 2007-08 in a little more detail.

CHAPTER TEN

The Anatomy of a Title-Winning Season (2007-08)

11 August 2007

We opened our League One campaign with a visit to the team that had pipped us for the final play-off position the previous season. Almost a quarter of the crowd at Boundary Park was from Swansea, with 1,645 Swans fans travelling to watch their team against Oldham Athletic. The home team scored after three minutes through a penalty converted by Michael Ricketts. Despite an equaliser by Jason Scotland in the second half, we lost 2-1, due to a goal in injury time by Welsh striker Craig Davies.

14 August 2007

For the Carling Cup First Round home tie against newly-promoted League One side Walsall I made seven changes to the team which had faced Oldham the previous Saturday. New signing Guillem Bauza and Liverpool loan signing

Paul Anderson made their first appearances. Anderson crowned his memorable evening with a goal and, another from substitute Jason Scotland gave the Swans a 2-0 passage into the next round to meet Premiership side Reading at the Liberty Stadium. The victory allowed us to see many new faces enjoying their football for Swansea City at the Liberty for the first time, one of them being goalkeeper Dorus De Vries, who showed great form.

18 August 2007

Nottingham Forest, the bookmakers' favourite to win the title, visited the Liberty Stadium for a league fixture. In one of our better home performances we were unable to score, despite Jason Scotland and Ferrie Bodde both hitting the post, and the game ended in a goalless stalemate. Forest's goalkeeper, Paul Smith, was outstanding between the posts achieving an impressive clean sheet which would be the third of the 26 that he would manage in the 2007/08 season.

25 August 2007

The Swans chalked up their first League One win with a second victory over Walsall in the space of eleven days. Goals in the Midlands heat from Jason Scotland and two from Andy Robinson, one of which was a penalty, gave us a 3-1 win. Although the sun made playing conditions difficult, I was glad for the new signings from abroad. At long last they could see that Britain does sometimes have a summer!

28 August 2007

A crowd of over 12,000, the highest in the second round of the Carling Cup, turned out to watch the Swans fight a highly-contested battle against Reading. After the scores ended level at full time we conceded the only goal of the match in the last minute of the first half of extra time. Man of the Match was a very young Joe Allen, who made his second competitive start with a commanding display full of quality and showing a maturity well above his years. A diamond of Welsh football with a fantastic future.

1 September 2007

Although not firing on all cylinders, after a forty-first minute goal by Jason Scotland we looked as if we were easing to a home victory over Doncaster Rovers. The balance of the game changed in the sixtieth minute when Ferrie Bodde was dismissed after an off-the-ball incident with Rovers' Brian Stock. With our ten men battling to hold onto a 1-0 lead, we were defeated by two late long-range strikes by Richard Wellens.

4 September 2007

The start of the Johnstone's Paint Trophy – a competition which we had won by beating Carlisle United at the Millennium Stadium in 2005. First up were Millwall. After two successive defeats at the hands of Reading and Doncaster Rovers, it was good to find the winning touch again. We were ahead after sixteen minutes through a Paul Anderson goal, but then, after fifty-three minutes, we were 2-1 down and the players had to show great character and responsibility to find the football solutions to win what turned out to be a superb match. Goals from Jason Scotland and an own goal saw us safely through to the next round with a 3-2 victory.

14 September 2007

In the league against Carlisle United we saved the best until last. Trailing 1-0 and with ten minutes to go, we stormed back to win 2-1 with goals from Darryl Duffy and Paul Anderson. It was a fantastic performance which showed all the ingredients of a winning team! Having to play a difficult role in the game after conceding a penalty in a rare attack from Carlisle, we displayed patience in our play to win the game.

18 September 2007

For the fourth time in our six league games, we came from

behind to beat Cheltenham at Whaddon Road. Having postponed the original fixture because of Warren Feeney, Shaun McDonald and Jo Allen being on international duty, we ran out 2-1 winners with goals from Jason Scotland and Andy Robinson in a sharp second half display after a slow first half.

22 September 2007

We were looking forward to the challenge of facing Leeds United at Elland Road after their impressive run of six successive victories, and in front of a Premiership environment with a large crowd as the club tried to claw back its fifteen point deficit for going into administration. Unfortunately, we played the occasion and not the game and didn't perform up to our standards, suffering a 2-0 reverse with goals from Jermaine Beckford and David Prutton. After that game we became a stronger team.

29 September 2007

Brighton and Hove Albion were the visitors for our landmark fiftieth league game at the Liberty Stadium. Sadly, there was no chance of celebrating our anniversary in style. A below par performance from us, and a well disciplined display from the visitors, resulted in a 0-0 stalemate. Despite an improved second half display from the boys, we were unable to break the deadlock.

2 October 2007

After the disappointing results against Leeds United and Brighton and Hove Albion, we came back with a 2-1 win at home against Swindon Town. Goals from Jason Scotland and Warren Feeney gave us the three points. The victory meant that we moved up into sixth place in League One. It was a hard fought result, with the fans giving us fantastic support. The group huddle at the end from the players meant a winning mentality and desire to succeed was starting to grow in the dressing room. A special chemistry started that night with the fans at the Liberty.

6 October 2007

Against the top team in the league and on their own ground, we put in a stunning performance to beat Leyton Orient. The 5-0 victory, with two goals from Tom Butler and one each from Darren Pratley, Paul Anderson and Warren Feeney, set a new record for an away win by a Swansea City team. It also sent out a huge message to the rest of the division and we had to be ready to deal with the expectations that that result would bring. After the match we moved to the top of the table above Tranmere Rovers and Orient.

9 October 2007

The second round of the Johnstone's Paint Trophy saw us

at home to Wycombe Wanderers. The previous season, the Chairboys had surprised everyone by reaching the semi-finals of the League Cup, so we knew we were in for a hard cup match. It was exciting to see Guillem (Bussy) Bauza score his first goal for the Swans, with Paul Anderson scoring the other in our 2-0 victory.

14 October 2007

Another top drawer performance this time at the Fitness First Stadium saw us win 4-1 against Bournemouth. Goals by Ferrie Bodde, Denis Lawrence and two from Warren Feeney kept us at the top of the table.

20 October 2007

We were due to play Hartlepool United at the Liberty Stadium, but the match was called off due to the tragic death the night before the game of their twenty-year-old winger, Michael Maidens. We rearranged the game for November 27 and, along with my assistant, Graeme Jones, and club chaplain, Kevin Johns, I visited the Hartlepool players at their Swansea hotel to express our support and condolences over their dreadful loss.

27 October 2007

Our away game at Huish Park against Yeovil Town was a potentially difficult trip. In four previous trips we had never picked up a point or a goal. For me, personally, it was also an interesting challenge, as it was on this ground that I had watched the Swans for the first time as their manager in the 2006-07 season. With a performance of great character, cheered on by nearly fifteen hundred travelling fans, we chalked up a 2-1 victory, with goals from Angel Rangel and Ferrie Bodde. The win moved us into second place, having lost ground through not playing the previous week. The result also ended a wonderful month for us. We won every one of our five games that October, four of which were in the league.

2 November 2007

After the great form of October, we found ourselves 1-0 down at home to Gillingham after a tenth minute wonder strike by Delroy Facey. Fifteen minutes later, we were reduced to ten men when Warren Feeney was sent off. At half time, I asked the boys whether they wanted to go back out there and win the game or just accept that it was a bad day at the office. Their answer was obvious for everyone to see. Although we only drew through a late Paul Anderson equaliser, the performance was appreciated by the crowd. The point put us back on top of the table, briefly, until all the rest of the chasing pack played the following day. In injury time, we almost won the game and all three points. After Leon Britton was brought down in the penalty box, Andy Robinson stepped up to take the penalty, but it was saved, as was the follow up shot by Gills' goalkeeper, Simon Royce. The draw felt like a win.

6 November 2007

Never having won at Millwall's Den in seventy-seven years, perhaps a 2-2 draw was a good result. It extended our unbeaten run to eight games and moved us up a place to fourth spot in the table. However, at the end of the game, we were all disappointed, as we knew we could have played better. Goals from Jason Scotland and Paul Anderson secured the point. Their second goal from the penalty spot was questionable. Kevin Austin, who was penalised, was one yard away from the cross, so it couldn't possibly have been a handball.

10 November 2007

With a break from league action, we went into the magic world of the FA Cup. As the favourites to progress against Billericay Town, we were in a no-win situation. Our opponents were just two points above the relegation zone in the Rymans League when they entertained us at their New Lodge ground. Despite their lowly position, they played a fantastic game, pushing us all the way. Trailing 1-0 for over thirty minutes, we finally pegged Billericay back and won 2-1, with Guillem Bauza scoring both our goals as he tasted the magic of the FA Cup for the first time.

13 November 2007

Three days after the trip to Essex, we were in cup action again, this time at home to Yeovil Town in the Johnstone's Paint Trophy. Guillem found the net again and his only goal of the game meant that we progressed into the Southern Area semi-final.

16 November 2007

We missed the chance to go top by losing 1-0 at home to Huddersfield Town in the league. Gary Monk had what seemed to be a perfectly good goal disallowed during injury time. I was disappointed by our performance and also by the fact that our run of ten games without defeat had come to an end, but this defeat changed our performance levels at home for the rest of the season with a clear change in our approach. A definite turning point in our season.

24 November 2007

A disciplined performance at Prenton Park got us back to our winning ways, as we defeated Tranmere Rovers with a deflected own goal. This was a very tough fixture and we had to work extremely hard for the three points.

27 November 2007

In the rearranged match against Hartlepool United we ran out 1-0 winners, thanks to a magnificent goal from

Angel Rangel. Even though Angel's performances had been outstanding all season, he didn't always get the praise he deserved. His first goal for the club helped to bring to everyone's attention what an outstanding player he is. It also put us back on top of League One.

30 November 2007

All week the Press were full of predictions that our visit to Horsham in the second round of the FA Cup was a potential banana skin. On the day, the weather was atrocious, as was the pitch, and the game should never have gone ahead. I'm sure that, if it hadn't been live on Sky TV, the game would have been postponed. Guillem Bauza scored yet another cup goal for us, and we held on to the 1-0 lead until the last few minutes when they were awarded a penalty, which they converted for a 1-1 draw. The decision was a disgrace, but I suppose it was all part of the occasion. I suspect that the referee would never have given the penalty in the eighty-fifth minute if it were not an FA Cup tie match for a non-league team against a league team being televised live. I suppose it was good drama for the three hundred and seventy thousand viewers who were watching the match on TV.

4 December 2007

The last month of the year got off to the best possible start for us with a superb performance in our 3-0 home defeat of Northampton Town. It was a win which opened up a two-point gap, as we consolidated our position on top of the table. In many games at the Liberty Stadium we had been unable to break down teams, but in this game we played with width and purpose and gained our largest victory at home. Two goals from Jason Scotland and the other from Darren Pratley earned us maximum points.

10 December 2007

The first ever FA Cup match at the Liberty Stadium saw us come from 1-0 down to beat Horsham in the replay 6-2. Darren Pratley, Leon Britton, Jason Scotland, Ferrie Bodde, Andy Robinson and Warren Feeney scored the goals, to give us a home tie against Havant and Waterlooville in the Third Round.

15 December 2007

We took three points and scored three goals against Southend United, a side strongly tipped at the start of the season for a quick return to the Championship. Goals from Warren Feeney, Angel Rangel and Tom Butler gave us the victory in a game which we controlled from beginning to end and in which we played with great style. The only black spot on a fabulous afternoon was that Warren Feeney was stretchered off with an ankle ligament injury.

26 December 2007

The first Boxing Day match at the Liberty Stadium saw us pit our wits against Cheltenham Town, a team which, throughout its stay in League One, was always likely to grab the headlines with outstanding results against top teams. With them having beaten us 2-1 at home the previous season, we expected a difficult battle. As it turned out, we gave another vintage December performance to win 4-1 with goals from Ferrie Bodde, Jason Scotland and two from Andy Robinson.

29 December 2007

A crowd of nearly twenty thousand turned out for our home match against Leeds United, the giants of League One. Throughout history, there have been strong links between the two clubs, with Alan Curtis having played for both teams and the fact that Leeds United folk hero, John Charles, was Swansea born. Another link is that, after Swansea City were promoted to the top division for the first time in their history, their first home game was against Leeds United, with the Swans winning 5-1. While we couldn't replicate the scoreline, the boys gave another breathtaking display, winning 3-2, despite being reduced to ten men for an hour of the game. Andy Robinson, Gary Monk and Jason Scotland scored our goals.

1 January 2008

2008 was heralded in with a 1-1 draw at the County Ground, Swindon. After twenty minutes they had a player sent off, and I think that once they went down to ten men, they played very defensively and killed the game. With just three minutes of normal time left, Tom Butler scored. Then, seven minutes into injury time, they equalised through a dubious penalty.

5 January 2008

With things going so well in the league, it was back to cup duty with two successive games. The first was in the third round of the FA Cup. For the third time in a row we were drawn against a non-league club, but at least the tie against Havant and Waterlooville was at home. It was a tough and rough game. We dominated throughout, with Jason Scotland, Leon Britton and Darren Pratley all hitting the bar. Havant and Waterlooville's Brett Poate was sent off for an horrendous tackle on Andrea Orlandi. In the scuffle that followed, Alan Tate was also sent off. Then, with three minutes to go to the final whistle, they scored. Things didn't work out for us. On another day we could have been two or three goals ahead going into the closing stages.

8 January 2008

Just three days later, we were in cup action at home once

again. This time the opponents were Brighton and Hove Albion in the Johnstone's Paint Trophy southern semi-final. We won 1-0. I was thrilled that the goal was scored by Darryl Duffy. He had been feeling down because, although a striker, he hadn't been scoring goals. But in this game all his hard work on the training ground came to fruition. Once we were 1-0 in front, Brighton and Hove Albion came back strongly. Dorus de Vries made some great saves, and we deservedly progressed to the regional final.

12 January 2008

Sporting our new away strip of green and black, we returned to league duty at Kenilworth Road to play Luton Town. Luton were fighting for their lives, having slipped into the relegation zone after a ten point deduction for going into administration. They fought tenaciously, but I thought we played extremely well, with some clinical finishing giving us a 3-1 victory through goals by Guillem Bauza, Jason Scotland and an own goal created by good work from Andy Robinson.

16 January 2008

As we took to the field away to Havant and Waterlooville for our FA Cup third round replay, we knew that victory would lead to an away tie with Liverpool. Despite goals by

Guillem Bauza and Jason Scotland, it was not to be and we lost 4-2.

19 January 2008

After the devastation of the cup exit, it was vital that we bounced back in our home league match against Port Vale. We came through the test with flying colours, but I was concerned at half time that we were only leading 1-0 through Ferrie Bodde's goal. In the second half, the boys showed how much they wanted to win, and their supremacy was reflected in the goal scored by Darren Pratley which gave us a 2-0 win. Darren's goal was the 100th Swans goal at the Liberty Stadium.

22 January 2008

Our 2-1 home victory over Crewe Alexandra was another example of dominating a game with fast flowing football. The scoreline didn't reflect the performance and the fact that we had 24 attempts on goal and 17 corners. It was our seventh successive home win, secured by goals from Tom Butler and Paul Anderson, taking us eight points clear at the top of the table.

25 January 2008

The visit to an in-form Doncaster Rovers was our fifth game in thirteen days. Rovers brought the game forward to Friday night because the club needed the car park on the Saturday for a race meeting! The boys showed tremendous personality and commitment with another great performance which earned us a 4-0 victory, with goals from Ferrie Bodde, Guillem Bauza, Jason Scotland and Febian Brandy. The victory put us eleven points clear at the top.

29 January 2008

Just four days after the tough visit to Doncaster, we took another potentially difficult trip, this time to the City Ground to face Nottingham Forest. In front of twenty-one thousand fans, we earned an excellent 0-0 draw. This time we used our past lessons and adapted well to play our game and to be ourselves on a very difficult occasion.

2 February 2008

A lot of tired bodies took to the field for our home fixture against Oldham Athletic. Having gone ahead through an own goal in the sixty-seventh minute, we conceded an equaliser eight minutes later. With the minutes ticking away, Febian Brandy, who had come on as a substitute, scored the winner in our 2-1 victory with five minutes to spare. The victory meant we had a ten point lead at the top of the table.

9 February 2008

Away to Crewe Alexandra, we became victims of our own success. Ahead 2-0 at half time, we were in total control and seemed to be coasting towards victory. Then we made uncharacteristic mistakes and conceded two goals, one of them in the last minute. Crewe's comeback wiped out the two goal advantage we had gained through a Jason Scotland goal and an own goal, so we came away with a 2-2 draw.

12 February 2008

With a 1-0 home victory over Walsall we made sure that the point gained at Crewe was a good one not a bad one. We limited Walsall to just one shot on target. Ferrie Bodde's goal, which was a wonderful strike from twenty-five yards, gave us the win. This was our third victory over Walsall in the season. It was a very dominant and pleasing performance and just for the record, yet another missed penalty at home.

16 February 2008

Our visit to Port Vale found us under pressure for the first twenty-five minutes. The home side were bottom of the table before the match, and in that first period of the game they showed that they were fighting for their lives. I was thrilled by the way the boys withstood the pressure, and Dorus de Vries made some wonderful saves to give us a platform on which to build. A converted penalty by Jason Scotland and a goal from Ferrie Bodde gave us a 2-0 victory and enabled us to extend our unbeaten run to sixteen games in the league.

19 February 2008

We were back in cup action, at home to MK Dons, with the first leg of the Johnstone's Paint Trophy southern final. Unfortunately, we gave away a sloppy goal in the second half and lost 1-0. Although I was disappointed with the performance and the result, I knew at the end that it was a one hundred-and-eighty-minute game and we still had a chance to put things right. To reach this point we had expended a lot of effort and minutes of football and the game could have been decided in the first 15 minutes where we enjoyed some glorious chances.

22 February 2008

A 1-0 home victory over Luton Town came courtesy of a fantastic solo goal by Tom Butler. In this game, I believe he showed that he was a potential Premiership League player playing in League One. His stylish seventy-ninth minute goal enabled us to open a huge fourteen point gap at the top of the table. It also meant that we were undefeated in seventeen games and it helped us pass the seventy point barrier.

25 February 2008

In the second leg of the Johnstone's Paints Trophy southern final we produced a very positive display with plenty of chances but we could only win the game to draw level on aggregate. The lottery of penalties sent the MK Dons to the final. It was disappointing for everyone connected to Swansea City to come so close to an appearance at the new Wembley, but the dressing room soon became focused on putting the disappointment behind us and driving forward to the league title.

1 March 2008

We marked St David's Day with a 1-0 victory against Huddersfield Town at Galpharm Stadium, a venue where we had not won in the last four visits. Jason Scotland scored in the first half of injury time to give our loud travelling fans something to celebrate. We could also celebrate our recovery after the setback of the previous Monday night at Milton Keynes and the fact that we were fourteen points clear of the other teams in the league. After the match, we left for a midweek football break in Spain.

7 March 2008

Before our home game with Millwall, the Press made much of the fact that if we came out of the game undefeated we would equal a thirty-seven-year-old club record of 19 games without defeat. As far as I was concerned making and breaking records was not our priority. The important thing for us as a team was to progress in to the next level of the league. After twenty-eight seconds, the record looked fairly unattainable when Millwall scored an early goal. With thirty minutes remaining, they stretched their lead further. Three minutes later, we pulled a goal back through Jason Scotland's converted penalty. Although we camped in their half for the rest of the match and put them under pressure, we could not find the equaliser.

11 March 2008

An equaliser in the last minute of our home game against Tranmere Rovers saw us draw 1-1, after we had led from the forty-third minute with a goal by Alan Tate. In any campaign you will go through a tough time and I told the boys they mustn't get downhearted. We had to see it as one more point to our projected tally for the season and our hoped-for promotion to the Championship. From time to time, football will hit you with harsh blows and this was one of them.

15 March 2008

Our 4-2 away defeat at the hands of Northampton Town was our heaviest reverse of the season. After thirty minutes we had conceded three soft goals. It was as if we had forgotten the intensity of our play, and when you are at the top of the league you must be prepared to maintain certain high standards in your play because every opposition will treat the game as a cup final and there is no margin of error. For the last hour of the game, I thought we showed great attitude but, despite two goals by Jason Scotland, we were unable to claw back such a huge deficit. Despite the heavy defeat, we remained six points clear at the top, as Doncaster Rovers lost and Carlisle drew.

18 March 2008

After the disappointment at the Sixfields Stadium, Northampton, the boys returned to form with a 2-0 win against Bristol Rovers at the Memorial Stadium. On a difficult playing surface which is also used for rugby, they showed great character and goals from Denis Lawrence and Jason Scotland sealed the points. The performance demonstrated great determination and restored a nine point lead at the top.

21 March 2008

For our third successive away game we visited Southend United at Roots Hall. As they had made a late surge into the play-off positions, we knew it was going to be a tough fixture. Jason Scotland put us ahead in the twenty-third minute with a classy touch from the penalty spot. They then equalised in the fifth minute of injury time at the end of the first half, when I think we should all have been back in the dressing room. I thought our back five played superbly, and we had to see it as a point gained rather than two lost.

24 March 2008

We were back at the Liberty Stadium at last, to meet Bristol Rovers for the second time in six days. With fifteen thousand fans roaring us on, and the Sky TV cameras present, it was all set for one of our great performances. At half time we were 2-0 down and I'd say that our first forty-five minutes were as bad as we had been all season. Then for the second forty-five minutes we were close to our best, showing the true face of Swansea City. Two goals from Jason Scotland, which brought his goal tally for the season to 28, gave us a 2-2 draw. If people had tuned in to watch the second half on their TV sets, I don't think they would have thought they were watching a League One game. The standard of our play was much higher.

29 March 2008

We made another long trip on the road, this time to Victoria Park, to play Hartlepool United. With just twenty-six seconds on the clock, we found ourselves trailing 1-0, but the boys fought back brilliantly and two goals from

Darren Pratley and one from Jason Scotland gave us a 3-1 victory. As Carlisle were held to a 0-0 draw by Gillingham, we stretched our lead at the top to seven points. It was a fantastic achievement by the team to be going into April with eighty-two points on the board.

5 April 2008

We always do things the hard way at Swansea City. Our home game against Bournemouth was no exception to that general rule. With ninety minutes on the clock, we seemed to be home and dry and promoted, thanks to Andy Robinson's fiftieth minute goal. Then, within a two minute period of injury time, the visitors scored twice to give them a lifeline in their battle against relegation and put our promotion party on hold.

8 April 2008

We picked up a point from a 0-0 draw at Brunton Park against our near rivals Carlisle United but we deserved more than a point. It was a pleasure to watch the squad perform and stamp their authority on a very difficult ground. Carlisle tried to create an intimidating atmosphere and we reacted extremely well showing great composure and concentration in our play. I took it as a compliment that a team which was chasing us to the top spot felt they needed to be that physical.

12 April 2008

Promoted at last! Our 2-1 victory at the Priestfield Stadium in Gillingham saw us win promotion to Championship level for the first time in twenty-four years. Trailing 1-0, we scored twice just before half time with both goals coming from Guillem Bauza. At the end we partied with the fifteen hundred Swans fans who had travelled with us. I understand there were similar scenes of jubilation at the Liberty Stadium, where two thousand fans watched the match beamed into the hospitality lounges. Great emotional moments for our fans in our "new" home.

19 April 2008

Despite Andy Robinson's goal, we lost 2-1 at home to Yeovil. It was a strange experience because, although we lost the game, results elsewhere meant that we won the League One title. So, within seven days we had won promotion and the title. It was an opportunity for us to celebrate with the eighteen thousand fans inside the Liberty Stadium and to thank them for being the twelfth man in all our games. Their fantastic support had made a difference to us and helped us through many tricky games.

26 April 2008

Our 4-1 victory at home to Leyton Orient gave us the chance to play with relish and freedom. It was a great performance, and, although we still didn't have a trophy to show off, we celebrated at the end with our unique fans. Great feelings in the Liberty, celebrating the first promotion in the Stadium – a great chapter in the club's history.

3 May 2008

The final game of a long and exciting season. We came away from Brighton and Hove Albion's ground with a 1-0 victory and a trophy!

And now for the Championship ...

Kicking Every Ball is just one of a whole
range of publications from Y Lolfa.
For a full list of books currently in print,
send now for your free copy of our new
full-colour catalogue. Or simply surf into
our website

www.ylolfa.com

for secure on-line ordering.

TALYBONT CEREDIGION CYMRU SY24 5AP
e-mail ylolfa@ylolfa.com
website www.ylolfa.com
phone (01970) 832 304
fax 832 782